SEX EDUCATION

A Parent's Guide

ara Frost-
Sharratt

Sex Education – A Parent's Guide is also available in accessible formats for people with any degree of visual impairment. The large print edition and eBook (with accessibility features enabled) are available from Need2Know. Please let us know if there are any special features you require and we will do our best to accommodate your needs.

First published in Great Britain in 2012 by
Need2Know
Remus House
Coltsfoot Drive
Peterborough
PE2 9BF
Telephone 01733 898103
Fax 01733 313524
www.need2knowbooks.co.uk

Contents

Introduction

As a parent, educating your growing child about sex and relationships is one of the toughest and most important jobs you'll ever do. You have to inform in an impartial way, whilst still offering the benefit of your personal experience, and you also have to warn your kids of the dangers, without terrifying them. Your children need different information at different stages, they need constant reassurance and you will need nerves of steel and the patience of a saint to get them through puberty. But, if you're honest, open and always available to talk, you'll make your job so much easier.

If you bury your head in the sand and simply avoid the conversations, then you and your child will drift apart. Children and teens often live separate lives to their parents, with modern technology putting up barriers that see many parents oblivious to what their kids get up to outside the house (and more often than not, inside it as well). Ignoring the issues of sex and relationships won't make them magically disappear; it will just mean you are less well informed and less aware of your teen's sexual development.

Discussing sex and relationships is a healthy way to build a bond with your child, to develop a mutual trust and openness that can be beneficial for every aspect of family life. Despite the sullen looks, the slamming bedroom doors and the one-syllable answers to questions, your teen does want to talk to you. They might have a funny way of showing it most of the time, but you need to bear in mind that you are the adult and they are the child. You have the benefit of life experience, sexual experience, first love, first heartbreak and worries about personal development. You can impart this valuable information and share your knowledge with them.

As parents, you provide the foundation for your child's moral and emotional education. Their first experiences of love, affection and respect will be gleaned from their family set-up so it's up to you to set a good example; to ensure they feel loved and respected; that they are encouraged to display individuality; and that they never feel too embarrassed or scared to talk to you about anything.

'Despite the sullen looks, the slamming bedroom doors and the one-syllable answers to questions, your teen does want to talk to you.'

Many people feel that talking about sex from an early age encourages sexual experimentation and promiscuity but, in fact, the opposite is true. Sexual awareness and enlightenment brings with it a certain degree of maturity and the ability to stand back from a situation and assess it with clarity and confidence. Knowledge is power in all areas of life, and knowledge about sex and relationships is no exception.

This book is divided into easy-to-read chapters, breaking down every aspect of sex and relationship education, and how you, as a parent, can help to steer your child towards sensible choices as they reach puberty, mature, and begin to engage in sexual activity. You will learn about techniques for dealing with difficult conversations, how to fill in the gaps between the national curriculum and real life; and how you can support your child in their choices and help them deal with any problems they encounter.

Need2Know

Chapter One

Let's Talk About Sex

Good parenting is a result of a number of factors, but one of the most important roles you have, as a parent, is to ensure effective communication between you and your children. This begins with facial expressions, nursery rhymes and baby talk but soon moves on to conveying to your child their place in the world and offering constant security, reassurance and discipline through the conversations you have with them.

As children get older, they'll have more questions and these questions will inevitably involve discussing where they came from and how they were made. There will come a point when you need to talk about sex with your child and this may well fill you with a sense of dread or anticipation. But there are ways of going about it that will make the experience stress-free for you, as well as being useful and informative for your child.

Why it can be embarrassing to talk about sex

If you've developed an open and honest relationship with your child, then the inevitable questions about sex and relationships should be a natural part of their development and growth. After all, if no one had sex, the human race would have had a very brief stay on the planet. But however open-minded and approachable you are, discussing the facts of life can still be embarrassing for both parties.

'As children get older, they'll have more questions and these questions will inevitably involve discussing where they came from and how they were made.'

Mum and Dad are doing it

The time that children become aware of the biological details of sex is the same time they realise exactly how they were created. Kids' reactions to the idea of their parents having sex varies from hilarity to distaste, so it's understandable that this can create a barrier to discussions. But, instead of getting embarrassed, try and use this to focus the conversation: a way of discussing how sex is a perfectly natural and important part of a loving relationship.

The big taboo

Sex is generally seen as a taboo subject and children tend to be sheltered from it to a certain extent. This is what results in playground talk of mythical proportions and it can lead to confusion and misconceptions about all issues of a sexual nature. That's why it is so important to ensure you're prepared for the sex and relationship conversations with your child whenever they feel the need to talk.

What is sex and relationship education?

Sex and relationship education (SRE) covers a very broad spectrum of topics and these can crop up in everything from science to personal development. Although the factual nature of sex education is essential for children to get a basic understanding of how their bodies work, teaching has developed to ensure a cohesion between the physical facts and the emotional side of relationships. By incorporating issues of feelings and emotions, children begin to develop an awareness of how sexual relationships can affect them as an individual, as well as the other people involved.

The facts are obviously important, but facts alone cannot prepare children for sexual encounters. They need to be aware of the responsibilities that come with sexual development, as well as the health risks involved in having unprotected sex, and how to prevent unwanted pregnancy. The idea is to promote understanding and knowledge, in order to encourage teens to delay sexual activity until they are physically and emotionally able to handle the situation. There are strict guidelines in place for SRE in schools (see page 19), although individual schools do have a great deal of autonomy in how and when they teach SRE.

Developing skills

Sex education knowledge will give your child the confidence to make more informed choices. Armed with the facts, he or she won't need to rely on second-hand information from their peers, which will more than likely be exaggerated at best and dangerously inaccurate at worst.

The fact that children have this knowledge doesn't mean that they will act upon it. On the contrary, sex education will give them the confidence and awareness to make safer choices. It will empower them, as they will be fully aware of the potential pitfalls of embarking on a sexual relationship. The choice to have sex or to wait is more likely to be a decision entirely of their own making, as they will have the facts at their disposal and won't enter into a sexual encounter naively, or under the misguided information from peers or partners.

Why talking is so important

Children learn about sex from their peers, from their parents, from school, and from the vast array of media sources that surround them. As a parent, you're always going to be their most reliable source of information, as you have their best interests at heart. They might find it easier to pick up bits and pieces of information overheard at school, but if you want them to be well informed and able to make sensible choices about sex and relationships, then talking to them is the best option.

Make time to talk

One of the best ways to ensure they feel comfortable talking about their concerns or asking questions is to keep lines of communication open. No matter how busy you are, try to stop and chat to your child when they ask. Kids like to add to their knowledge base with snippets of information, gradually building up the whole picture. If you pass up on an opportunity to talk, they might not ask next time. It can take a lot of courage to ask tricky questions: always be ready to answer them.

'The fact that children have this knowledge doesn't mean that they will act upon it.'

The evidence for sex education in the home

There are so many reasons why discussing sex at home with your kids is a good idea. Aside from providing them with honest answers to awkward questions, you're reiterating the fact that they're part of a loving family that cares about them and wants the best for them.

Setting the standards

A healthy attitude towards sex can form the basis for relationships that kids have later on in life. By understanding sexual relationships from an adult perspective, kids can begin to entertain notions about love, mutual respect and faithfulness. As they get older and start to have their own relationships, they should have a good grounding about what to expect from a partner in terms of respect and honesty.

'Children tend to ask the questions that relate directly to them and their place in the world at different stages of their development.'

Although this isn't always going to be the reality, if they enter into a new relationship on these terms they can very quickly determine whether they are being treated well by a partner. Whether they choose to continue with an unrewarding or one-sided relationship is up to them; but at least they will be aware of the parameters and understand that a successful relationship results from mutual respect. If they are aware of the basic values of meaningful and lasting relationships, they will become more discerning about the choices they make about partners.

It's never too early to have the conversation

Children tend to ask the questions that relate directly to them and their place in the world at different stages of their development. As babies turn to toddlers, they begin to have a sense of self and see themselves as having a defined place in the family unit. It's only natural that, as they grow older, they start to question how they arrived in the world, how they were made and where they came from. Their honesty, innocence and total acceptance of what you tell them make it important to answer their questions in a way that will appease, rather than frighten or confuse them. Whilst the notion of the stork delivering new babies kept a whole generation of children blissfully ignorant of the facts of life, they no doubt got an almighty shock when they finally learnt about the reality of childbirth.

Relate to their world

Young children love games so you could use teddies or dolls to explain about babies growing in their mummy's tummy. Always base the information you give on the age and personal development of your child, providing just enough information to answer their questions, without confusing them.

Siblings

If a new sibling arrives in the household, or a close friend or relative has a new baby, this can often provoke questions. It can also be a good time to have the first conversations about where babies come from. There's no need for detailed descriptions or drawn-out explanations – a pregnant tummy followed by a new baby will be sufficient explanation for an inquisitive toddler.

Building on their knowledge

If children have been given basic information from a young age, it will be far easier to add more detail as they get older and have more probing questions about sex. If you make a point of always being honest with them, they will hopefully always come to you first and you can make sure they have accurate information. It's far better to add to their knowledge base gradually than to have one almighty 'facts of life' conversation at some point in the future. What kids don't know, they will make up for themselves or collate from other unreliable sources: far better to give answers that you've tailored for their age and awareness than to have them worried or confused about things they have overheard in the playground.

Talking doesn't encourage doing

It's a common misconception that talking about sex and being open about it from a young age will encourage promiscuity and teenage pregnancy. In fact, the opposite is true: if a child is well informed about the physical and emotional implications of embarking on a sexual relationship, they'll be far better equipped to make an informed choice when the issue arises. Ignorance certainly isn't bliss when you're on the brink of a sexual encounter and you have no idea about contraception, conception, STIs or the confidence to say 'no' if you're not ready. A survey revealed than an astonishing 99% of children believe that talking about sex wouldn't encourage them to have sex. (*Populus, June 2008*)

Be honest

Kids will respect your honesty and you should offer them the same courtesy. If your child comes to you looking for advice, try and act as an impartial voice. You should feel proud that you've created an environment that encourages them to discuss sexual issues, rather than bottling them up or turning to friends. The notion of sexually promiscuous teenagers can make some parents shy away from bringing up the subject, but sexual awareness will give your child greater power, independence and confidence as they grow and develop.

'If your child comes to you looking for advice, try and act as an impartial voice.'

The best sex education is . . .

There is no right or wrong when it comes to sex education. As long as you are constantly aware of your child's increasing curiosity and answer their questions as honestly and frankly as you can, then you're doing the right thing. The time and place you choose to talk is irrelevant; questions can crop up anytime. Be prepared to offer advice about contraception while you're doing the school run, or to answer questions about genital warts while you prepare dinner.

Kids might want to have a quick chat then change the subject, or they might want a heart to heart – again, be prepared for every situation and circumstance and you can't go too far wrong. At the end of the day, the fact that your child is coming to you voluntarily to ask about sexual matters means that you're doing a good job. As they get older, you might want to pass on specific medical advice, in which case a visit to the sexual health clinic or the school nurse might be beneficial. It's good to keep up to date with the latest information about STIs and contraception, and again, your local health clinic will have leaflets and other information that you and your teen can take away and read.

Summing Up

- Keep lines of communication open.

- Be approachable, honest and impartial.

- Make sure you're never too busy to talk – kids don't always pick the best moments to ask questions.

- Keep sex education age appropriate, younger children just need the basics.

- Information is education and sex education is essential.

- Add to their knowledge base and don't be afraid to speak openly and candidly – sexual awareness doesn't lead to sexual promiscuity.

Chapter Two

What Do You Know?

Playground whispers

Young girls are petrified that they can get pregnant by kissing a boy, and many girls believe that they can't get pregnant the first time they have sex with a boy. Older boys spread rumours about being able to reuse condoms or withdrawing before ejaculation to avoid pregnancy. Whatever their age, you can be pretty certain that much of your child's school sex education is learnt in the playground, rather than the classroom. This makes it more important than ever to start talking about sex with your kids from an early age. You can dispel the myths and put them right about the facts.

Bravado and bragging

Kids love to think they're imparting pearls of wisdom to their peers and whether or not they know their claims are false, the fact that they can grab other children's attention, particularly when it comes to sex talk, means that playground banter will always be an issue. Children have their first sexual encounters at very different ages and these real and invented experiences are also the stuff of schoolyard legend, making it trickier for kids to get an accurate portrayal of sex. Regardless of how good sex and relationship education is at your child's school, they will eagerly soak up any titbits of information gleaned from huddled conversations by the bike sheds during lunch break.

'Whatever their age, you can be pretty certain that much of your child's school sex education is learnt in the playground, rather than the classroom.'

Find out the facts

If your kids open up to you and let you know what they've heard, you can gauge how much information you want to give them at any one time. If they're talking about unprotected sex in first break then it's probably time to have a serious conversation about contraception and STIs. Always allow them to take the initiative. You might be shocked by the topics of sex conversation that they're engaging in with their friends at different stages but it's better to put them straight about the facts, even if you think they're too young to be discussing certain issues. If they're thinking about it anyway, then that bubble of innocence has already been burst and you need to step into the breach to ensure that the information they're getting is accurate and realistic.

The Internet

The Internet has totally transformed the way we access information: we can look up any fact, celebrity story, news item or image at the click of a mouse. However, this instant access comes at a price. It is now far more difficult for parents to veto the information that their children watch or hear. Whether your kids are online actively seeking out pornography or any sexual content, or whether they have been coerced into watching it by their friends, there's one thing you can be sure of – they are watching it, and probably from a younger age than you imagine.

Easy access

From indecent images and explicit song lyrics to film clips, live Internet channels and porn chat rooms, kids today have constant and easy access to every level of gratuitous sexual and violent content that they care to access. This makes it more difficult for both kids and parents to gauge sexual awareness and maturity: there is no longer a natural progression to a child's sexual curiosity and development. With sexual content so readily available online, your child could be exposed to graphic sexual images and contradictory messages from a very young age.

'From indecent images and explicit song lyrics to film clips, live Internet channels and porn chat rooms, kids today have constant and easy access to every level of gratuitous sexual and violent content that they care to access.'

Mixed messages

A lot of pornography, by its very nature, could give children at a vulnerable age very mixed messages about a lot of sex and relationship issues. Their experience of the world at this stage is limited and they don't have any reference points to offer a comparison to scenes of sexual violence, female subordination or gratuitous sexual behaviour. This can lead to a very skewed view of relationships and it's something you need to be aware of, in order to rationalise what they've been exposed to, and to offer a more balanced view of how sexual relationships work in the real world.

The exploitation of women

Women are often portrayed in a derogatory manner in pornography, and overexposure can lead to confusion amongst young boys and girls. Before they reach maturity and gain sufficient world experience to form their own judgements and learn from their own experience and mistakes, young people take their cues from their parents, their teachers, their peers and – to a large extent – the media. If they are exposed to a constant drip feed of misogynistic ideas, through pornography or explicit music and music videos, it's only natural that this will have an impact on their own attitudes.

Everyone's different

Obviously, each child will react to pornography in a different way and there's no need to panic unduly if you think your child has been exposed to it. It doesn't mean they're going to act out any of the scenarios they've witnessed. However, pornography does tend to shatter the image of love, trust and understanding in sexual relationships, which parents try to instil in their children from a young age.

Online predators

As a parent, pornography isn't the only thing you need to be aware of concerning the Internet. The anonymity of the World Wide Web has made it a haven for paedophiles and sexual predators, who try to lure children into clever traps. They will commonly invent themselves as teenagers on chat rooms, using teen speak and contemporary cultural references to convince kids online that they're 'chatting' to a 15-year-old boy in his bedroom, when in actual fact, it's a 50-year-old man.

Although teens are becoming more wise to the tricks used by sexual predators to gain their friendship and trust, they can still be caught out by the compliments, the subtle grooming and the gradual escalation of explicit chat. Your teen might be tricked into posting photos, engaging in sexually explicit conversations or, at the extreme end of the spectrum, meeting up with the man (or woman) in person. You need to talk about the dangers of online grooming to your child before they are exposed to it. If they're clued up about the potential dangers and know the signs to look out for, they are less likely to be duped. If you are worried at *any* point, contact the police.

Gauging parental influence

You might think that by banning televisions or computers from your child's bedroom, you are protecting them from the evils of the Internet. If that's the case, it's time to get realistic – if your child's curiosity gets the better of them, they will find ways of satiating it. Their friends' parents might be more lenient with regards to online access or they might have Internet access on their phone. And as for the school playground? Mobile phone bans do little to stop the flow of pornography in the playground, so you really are fighting a losing battle when it comes to protecting their innocence and shielding them from hardcore pornography, or indecent films and images.

How your kids can help you

Conversations about sex need to be open and honest; your children need to feel confident that they'll get the answers they're looking for. It will help a great deal if your child can tell you how much they already know. This doesn't mean going into graphic detail about their perceived or actual knowledge of sexual encounters but if they can give you a rough idea of their level of understanding then you can tailor your conversations accordingly.

Don't make assumptions

You might assume that you don't need to start with the basics but sometimes kids need this information from their parents. They might have got mixed messages from the playground or the television and they'll be looking to you to clarify things for them. Likewise, there's no point going through the details of sexual intercourse if they learnt this in school years ago and are coming to you for advice on more complicated concerns regarding their sexual behaviour.

Ask as well as answer

Kids don't always want to be completely honest about how much they know and what their experience to date is. And you don't want to alienate them by asking questions that might embarrass them. But if you can turn the discussion into a two-way conversation, your child is more likely to open up. The more informed you are about their level of sexual knowledge and experience, the more you can help and advise them and the more likely you are to spot any potential problems.

Sex and relationship education (SRE) in schools

You might be surprised to discover that SRE varies widely between schools. Although there are certain guidelines in place about age-appropriate sex education and the topics that should be covered, the depth of the discussions and the extent that sex education is carried through to different areas of learning is really down to the governors of the school. Whilst SRE is largely taught in science lessons, the broader issues will be taught more informally in other subject areas, where appropriate. According to national guidelines published by DfES (Department for Education and Skills) in July 2000, your child should receive the following formal SRE, during primary and secondary school national curriculum science (summarised).

'You might be surprised to discover that SRE varies widely between schools.'

Key Stage 1

▪ Animals move, feed, grow and reproduce.

▪ Recognise main external parts of the human body.

▪ Learn that humans can produce offspring.

▪ Recognise similarities and differences between themselves and others.

Key Stage 2

▪ Human life processes including nutrition, growth and reproduction.

▪ Main stages of the human life cycle.

Key Stage 3

▪ Fertilisation in humans is the fusion of a male and female cell.

▪ Physical and emotional changes that occur during adolescence.

▪ Human reproductive cycle, including menstrual cycle and fertilisation.

▪ Bacteria and viruses can affect human health.

Key Stage 4

▪ Hormonal control in humans, including the effects of sex hormones.

▪ Medical uses of hormones.

▪ How sex is determined in humans.

Your role and rights in school SRE

Your child's school should keep you informed about the current policies of SRE and about exactly what is being taught. Parents do have the option to withdraw children from SRE lessons but not from compulsory science classes. Although some parents might have objections based on moral or religious grounds, it's a very drastic step to take and one that should be thought through very carefully. Formal SRE offers the basic foundation, and by denying your child access to this information, you are reducing their knowledge base and alienating them from their peers. Always discuss your decision with the school, as you might be required to demonstrate that you are taking steps to fill any gaps in their knowledge.

Don't leave it all to the school

Whilst SRE is more formalised these days, and children should benefit from a more proactive approach to preparing them for sexual activity, the information they receive in school is by no means exhaustive. Good teachers will be able to introduce elements of SRE into a number of different lessons but you should never assume that your child is getting all the information they need from this one source. You have an equal responsibility and the more they learn at school, the more questions they will inevitably have. Use formal SRE as a building block for their knowledge and be on hand to fill in the gaps, or to answer the tricky questions that they might be embarrassed to ask in front of their mates in the classroom.

Summing Up

- Warn them about the dangers online and how to avoid them.

- Be honest with your kids and ask them to be honest with you.

- Encourage them to share their knowledge and experiences.

- Never make assumptions about what your kids know or don't know.

- Be aware of Internet usage and be wise to pornography.

- Educate your kids about the realities of relationships as opposed to the one-dimensional views offered by porn films.

- Talk about the dangers of chat rooms and paedophiles.

- Keep up to date with the school policy on SRE.

- Use formal SRE as a building block, not an exhaustive resource.

Chapter Three

How to Talk About Sex and What to Discuss

Sex education starts early

'Where do I come from?' is the age-old question that shows a child is beginning to think about his or her place in the world. The way you answer this question will form the building blocks for the sex and relationship education that you provide for your child throughout their childhood and teenage years.

Children tend to ask questions at the most inappropriate moments. Unlike adults they don't consider waiting until an appropriate time and place. Instead, they will bombard you with questions as soon as they enter their head. So, don't be surprised if your 4-year-old asks where babies come from when you're sitting on a crowded bus or queuing at the supermarket.

'Children tend to ask questions at the most inappropriate moments.'

Keep your cool

You might be embarrassed and flustered but your child – and everyone around you – will be eagerly waiting for your response and watching to see how you deal with it. If you're going to set a precedent for future conversations and far more intimate questions, then try not to get flustered. Just answer the question as honestly and simply as you can, in terms that your child will understand. At an early age, it's fine to just explain that babies grow inside their mummy's tummy and come out when they're ready to see the world.

Ongoing conversations

If your child understands from early on that these discussions are a normal part of everyday life, then you've done the hard work already and that first question might well be the trickiest one you have to answer. A child will take their cue from you. If they see you getting tongue-tied, or bundling them away to somewhere out of earshot when they ask what is – to them – the most natural question in the world, then sex is going to seem like a taboo subject from a very early age.

Age-appropriate sex education

A child's perception of the world changes as they mature and develop, both physically and emotionally. Although they start asking questions from a very young age, it's important to keep their knowledge relevant to their age and their level of comprehension.

Obviously, every child is different and some children will be more curious about sex from an earlier age. Likewise, some children reach puberty at a much younger age than their peers, so all children need to be aware of the changes they're facing before they happen. As a very rough guide, these are the questions and topics that you might want to discuss with your children at different ages and the types of questions they might have:

Under 5

- Where do babies come from?

- How do babies get into mummies' tummies?

- How do they come out?

- The differences between girls and boys.

5-10

- Physical development – changes to their body.

- More details about conception and birth.

24

- Explaining that private parts are private.
- Correct names for girls' and boys' genitals.
- Menstruation (at the older end of the spectrum).
- Puberty (at the older end of the spectrum).

10-13

- Sexuality and same-sex relationships.
- Pregnancy and STIs.
- Masturbation.
- Erections.
- Wet dreams.

Answering embarrassing questions

It doesn't matter how well prepared and open-minded you are, there are bound to be certain questions or areas that you feel embarrassed discussing with your children, particularly when you're not expecting them. As mentioned briefly before, it is important to try and answer all your child's questions as honestly and plainly as possible.

Don't be shy

If you evade questions, then the innocent and naturally enquiring mind of the child will begin to associate certain aspects of sex and development as taboo. If this is the case, they might stop asking questions altogether. You will then have no control about the information they're getting and you're essentially leaving them to their own devices. However embarrassed you might be discussing masturbation or wet dreams with your child, wouldn't you rather be giving them truthful information than leaving it to misinformed teens or the Internet to provide their sex education?

'It doesn't matter how well prepared and open-minded you are, there are bound to be certain questions or areas that you feel embarrassed discussing with your children.'

Changing times

Puberty and sexual awakening can be frightening for a child if they're not fully prepared for the huge number of changes that their body is going to go through. If you have an 'open door' policy and your kids know they can come to you, even if the topic of conversation is an embarrassing one, you can quickly dispel myths or misinterpreted information that might otherwise worry and confuse them.

Keeping control of the conversation

If you are going to provide useful information for your child, you need to make sure that you stick to the subject. It's easy to waffle around the edges of a serious conversation about sex, but if you think there's something worrying your teen, or they have come to you for advice, then don't start off by talking about the weather. You might only have a brief window of opportunity while siblings are watching television or the dinner is in the oven and you need to take full advantage of it. If your child gets distracted, or loses their nerve to ask a particularly tricky question, then the moment has passed.

Keep them engaged

Try and get to the question as soon as possible. If they've been plucking up the courage to ask you something, you need to be on the ball and get them talking. Once they've told you what's bothering them, they will probably relax and then you can have a proper conversation. Try to stay focused on the actual topic and only move on to something else when the question has been answered. If you don't know all the facts (perhaps it's related to STIs or certain types of contraception), you should offer to go with them to a sexual health clinic to get more information.

Why your teens want to talk

Teenagers want to feel normal and they want to be liked by their peers. Puberty can often make kids feel confused and isolated. They might be shy about their developing bodies, or unsure if everything they are going through is normal.

They need your reassurance at this crucial stage in their lives more than ever. They are no longer children and yet they're still not adults: this transition puts a lot of pressure on teens and you can provide a huge amount of support.

But remember, your child does want to talk to you – whether they give that impression or not, they're desperate for accurate information from someone they trust implicitly. A survey found that 75% of 11 to 14-year-olds want to talk to their parents about sex but they just don't know how or when to bring it up in conversation (*Populus, June 2008*). This makes it all the more important for you to tune in to the signs that your child has something they want to talk about and that no topic is taboo.

Discussing relationships and dilemmas

A lot of teenagers have limited – or zero – experience of physical relationships and therefore the emotional side of sex. Whilst they have probably been bombarded with information – both factual and invented – by their friends, school and you, they will also need some understanding of the nature of relationships and how they work.

Getting emotional

It can often be more difficult discussing emotions with teenagers than it is to give them facts. Facts speak for themselves, but it's hard to understand potential emotional states and feelings if you have no concept or experience of them. However, for a rounded sex and relationship education, teens must at least have an idea of the unwritten rules of relationships and be prepared for some of the scenarios they might face once they start dating.

Respect and honesty

These are key to any successful relationship and it's important to talk to your teen about having respect for their partner from the outset. Whilst teenage boys and girls are often desperate to regale their friends with their sexual antics, no one wants to overhear snippets of conversations about how their

'A survey found that 75% of 11 to 14-year-olds want to talk to their parents about sex but they just don't know how or when to bring it up in conversation.'
Populus, June 2008.

first date went or how far their boyfriend got with them on the sofa the night before. It's only natural to feel excited about first sexual experiences but their partner's feelings and reputation should be seen as the priority.

What if . . .

This is a good way to introduce certain dilemmas to your teen. Ask rhetorical questions to ensure they know what they would do, and who they would talk to, if they had a problem. Let them know that whatever happens, you'll always be there for them but you expect them to act sensibly and not to take any risks.

- What if you thought you had an STI?
- What if a partner discovered they had an STI?
- What if you thought you might be pregnant?
- What if a partner was pressuring you into having sex?

'Everyone needs to be aware of the potential dangers of having unprotected sex.'

Discussing pregnancy and STIs

Pregnancy and STIs are part and parcel of sexual relationships. Both scenarios can easily be avoided if your teen is knowledgeable and takes precautions, so make sure they are aware of contraception, symptoms of STIs and the seriousness of certain infections.

Leaflets

It's unlikely that you'll have an encyclopaedic knowledge of the symptoms and treatment of every STI, so it's a good idea to better inform yourself before you have the conversation with your teen. Doctors' surgeries and sexual health clinics will have plenty of up-to-date leaflets and information, which you can read and pass on to your teen. Whilst you don't want to scare them, everyone needs to be aware of the potential dangers of having unprotected sex. When condoms are so readily available, there's no excuse for taking the risk and this is one of the best pieces of advice you can pass on to your teen.

Getting pregnant

Whether you have a son or a daughter, an unplanned pregnancy can put a huge strain on a family. Once again, you need to set the scene for any potential scenarios. Sexual relationships carry a certain amount of responsibility and teenagers can be ill-equipped to deal with the intense emotional and physical feelings that they experience. Contraception is such an important issue to discuss that it's not something to be casually brought up once or twice – this needs to be repeated and your teen needs to have all the information to be sexually active safely.

For more information on STIs take a look at *Sexually Transmitted Infections – The Essential Guide* and for more on pregnancy have a look at *Teenage Pregnancy – The Essential Guide* – part of the Need2Know series.

Exploding the myths about playground banter

Teens love to brag about their sexual encounters, and if your child believes everything they hear in the playground they might think they're the only kid on the block not having sex. You need to reassure them that often those who shout the loudest actually have the least to shout about. If your teen has a boyfriend or girlfriend, ask them how that person would feel if your teen was talking about them in a sexual way in front of everyone.

There's no hurry

Although many teenagers want to have their own tales to tell their mates and find out what all the fuss is about, it's important that they don't feel pressure to have sex before they're ready. A physical relationship will develop naturally and rushed sexual encounters might leave your teen feeling let down or disappointed. Talk to them about the benefits of delaying sex, the alternatives to penetrative sex and the emotional fulfilment of having sexual relations in the context of a loving relationship. Of course, your advice might fall on deaf ears but you can be there to pick up the pieces if they choose to ignore you.

Jumping to conclusions

Teenagers tend to have a bad reputation – they sulk, disappear off to their room for hours, disobey rules, grunt instead of talk, and they all apparently have sex all of the time. Well, actually, this last assumption is just as likely or unlikely to be as true as the others. Everyone's different and just because your teen has gone through puberty and takes an interest in the opposite sex (or the same sex), this doesn't mean they jump into bed with a partner every time you take your eyes off them.

Trust their judgement

Many teens don't have the confidence, experience, maturity or opportunity to engage in sexual relations, whilst others make a conscience decision to not rush into it before they're ready. Whilst it's true teenagers can act rashly and without consideration, isn't that the same for everyone? Given the right information and advice, teens will be able to make their own informed decisions about sex and you shouldn't make assumptions.

Keeping your judgments to yourself

Everyone has different views when it comes to sex and relationships, and your son or daughter won't necessarily share your opinions. From underage sex to abortion and promiscuity, there are going to be numerous occasions when your views vary greatly. The important thing is to learn to respect your teen's views, even if you don't agree with them. Ask them to do the same for you and then hopefully you can discuss all topics with an open mind.

If you allow your personal feelings to come into the conversation too much, your teen might shy away from telling you certain things. Try to be as open-minded as you can and remember, things change greatly with each generation so behaviour and actions that might have been looked down upon when you were a teenager could be perfectly acceptable amongst youngsters now. You're a parent, not a school teacher, and you need to be on your teen's side while still maintaining a sense of authority on the subject.

Showing your kids that you want to talk

The key to making sure your kids know you're keen to talk to them is to look out for the signs. If they're hanging around while you're getting dinner ready when they usually hibernate in their room, chances are they have something they want to ask. You know your own children better than anyone else does and you know their quirks and habits, so it's really a case of second-guessing them and being ready to chat at a moment's notice.

Clarifying facts

A kid's attention span is often hovering around zero so you need to pounce when you think they want to talk. Whatever you do, don't brush them off with, 'I'm busy', or 'I'll talk to you later'. By then the moment will probably have passed and you've lost your opportunity. Often kids will just want snippets of information. They might have heard something at school that's worrying or confusing them; maybe a friend has asked for advice about sex, or maybe they just need a bit of reassurance about a relationship or how to handle a tricky situation.

Plucking up the courage

Remember that your kids are probably more embarrassed than you about having conversations about sex. Although they might have caught you off guard when you're in the middle of a million and one jobs, they could have been working up to this particular moment for days and have finally plucked up the courage to ask you something that's of great importance to them.

Ready to talk checklist

- Look out for the signs that they want to talk.

- Let them know they have your undivided attention.

- Remember that most teens want to talk to their parents about sex.

- If the house is busy, go somewhere quiet to put them at ease: their bedroom is a place they feel secure.

'A kid's attention span is often hovering around zero so you need to pounce when you think they want to talk.'

- Keep eye contact and encourage them to talk frankly.
- Don't judge their or their friends' behaviour; try to offer sensible, impartial advice.
- Let them know they can come to you any time about anything.

Confidentiality

If your child comes to you in confidence with concerns about themselves or a friend, they need to know that they can talk to you candidly and openly. Whatever you do, don't betray that confidence. If they overhear you talking about their issues on the phone to someone, you will have shattered their trust and they're less likely to come to you next time they need advice.

Make a promise

Becoming sexually active is a huge part of a young person's development and it can trigger all kinds of emotional reactions, which they probably won't be prepared for. If your child needs your help, try to remove yourself from your role as a parent – just briefly – in order to give unbiased and truly helpful advice. Of course, you'll have their best interests at heart, and it's tough for every parent to watch the transition from child to adult, and all that it entails. But, if you want them to keep returning for your advice, they need to know that advice is impartial and of real value.

Summing Up

- Children will start asking questions from a very young age: answer them honestly, in terms they understand.

- Seize the moment – talk when they want to talk.

- Puberty can make a child vulnerable, emotional and lacking in confidence: your job is to reassure and inform.

- Talk to your teens about emotions as well as sexual facts.

- Dispel the myth of the playground bragger: most teens have little to brag about and exaggerate their experiences.

- If they talk to you in confidence, respect their request.

Chapter Four

Biology and Mechanics

Puberty

Puberty happens to boys and girls at different ages (between 10 to 15 years for boys, and 8 to 13 years for girls) and to each individual child at a different age. It's impossible to predict when your child is going to hit puberty, which is why it's so important that they're adequately prepared for these monumental changes to their body. If they know the facts from a fairly young age, when the changes do start to happen, they will hopefully be more inquisitive than alarmed and they will be better mentally prepared to deal with puberty.

What happens when?

As mentioned, everyone reaches puberty at a different age. When your child's body is ready to develop into an adult body, the pituitary gland (which is a pea-sized gland at the base of the brain), releases hormones that trigger the relevant changes to the male or female body. Essentially, for boys this means that the testes begin to produce testosterone and, for girls, it means the ovaries will start to produce oestrogen. This then triggers the other physical signs of puberty – hair growth, voice changes, muscle development, penis growth and breast development.

Hormones and mood swings

With the rush of hormones and their bodies quite literally changing before their eyes, it's no surprise that youngsters and teenagers can be a bit crabby. Even though they know the process, it can be quite unnerving to see hair growing in new and unexpected places, breasts developing and voices cracking and

'With the rush of hormones and their bodies quite literally changing before their eyes, it's no surprise that youngsters and teenagers can be a bit crabby.'

squeaking at inopportune moments. It has been said that puberty occurs at the time in your life when you're least well equipped to deal with it emotionally, and it's certainly true that this barrage of physical changes can make teens sullen, reclusive, moody and overly emotional. The bad news for parents is that it goes on for a few years so be prepared and hunker down.

New problems

Boys and girls have their own specific problems to face during puberty but they'll probably all feel embarrassed by their bodies at some stage, as they try to keep up with the changes and adjust to their new shape and appearance. They might become self-conscious about their physical appearance, or try to cover up their bodies more than before. This is all completely natural and you just need to remember to give them the privacy they need and try not to make too big a deal of the changes.

Odd one out

In some ways, waiting for puberty can be almost as traumatic for your child as actually going through it. If your child is a late developer, they will have to watch as all their friends grow taller, fill out or become more muscular, and start to get attention from the opposite sex. As there can be years between the onset of puberty amongst peer groups, some kids will have to wait a while to catch up with their friends and this can cause embarrassment and distress. No one wants to be the odd one out, or to be excluded from conversations. You should try to reassure your child that everyone develops at a different stage and their body will go through the changes when it's ready to do so.

Grieving for their childhood

Your sweet-smelling, smooth-skinned angelic boy will most likely wake up one morning with a face full of spots and a bad case of body odour, whilst your carefree wisp of a girl will develop curves and transform into a woman before you can blink. These changes don't just affect the kids: they'll affect you as a parent just as acutely. Puberty spells the end of the innocent stage of early childhood and signifies that your kids are becoming more independent, more forthright and, in some ways, more distant.

You're no longer needed for all the day-to-day caring and, much as you might have bemoaned bath time and hair wash, or dashed into work late because you were patching up a wounded knee and administering cuddles, you'll feel a sense of sadness when your kids start locking the bathroom door and tending to their own wounds. Although they will still rely on you for their basic needs, puberty is the time when kids begin to turn into adults and that necessitates a certain degree of parental separation and independence. So, you might lose bedtime stories but you'll still be expected to have cupboards stocked with food and be ready to drop everything to give them a lift into town.

Sex

Whether or not they're actually having sexual relationships, you can be pretty sure that they're thinking about it. Puberty prepares the body for reproduction and, as all the various physical elements are being slotted into place, thoughts will naturally turn to the practicalities of sex. Teens will become more inquisitive, as their emotional psyche tries to race and catch up with their developing adult body.

It's a turbulent time as their emotional and physical states won't necessarily be in tune with each other. They could well be physically able to have sexual relationships (and to have to deal with the consequences of this) but not be emotionally prepared for the feelings that accompany them.

Pregnancy

With sex comes responsibility and your teen has to be prepared for this. Teenagers often think they're invincible, and they'll take risks that an adult would baulk at. They don't have the life experience or the responsibilities that adults rely upon to weigh up the consequences of their actions, or to take a step back from a situation before plunging ahead.

'Puberty is the time when kids begin to turn into adults.'

Obviously, you can't use a blanket approach – some teens have a sensible head on their shoulders and mature more quickly – but it's always best to err on the side of caution and assume that a teenager might act more rashly than an adult, particularly when it comes to sex. They need to fully appreciate that whilst unprotected sex might provide a few minutes of fun, an unwanted pregnancy will affect the mother and father for the rest of their lives, whatever choices they make.

Don't talk down

'Government figures show that in 2009, 7,158 girls under the age of 16 became pregnant and the figure for the under-18 age group was 38,259.'

ONS 2011

There's no need to be patronising or reiterate the fact that they're not an adult yet. Speak to your teen on equal terms and try to impart the wisdom of your experience without creating such a wide generational gap that you alienate them. They know that unprotected sex can lead to pregnancy but check on their knowledge and make sure they aren't taking unnecessary risks like withdrawing before ejaculation; using a condom more than once; or relying on ECPs (emergency contraceptive pill).

Facing facts

The UK still has one of the highest rates of teenage pregnancy in Europe, and the highest rate of teenage birth and abortion in Western Europe (*United Nations Statistics Division, 2009*) so the message still isn't getting through and it's up to parents to make sure their teens are knowledgeable about the facts. Government figures show that in 2009, 7,158 girls under the age of 16 became pregnant and the figure for the under-18 age group was 38,259 (*ONS 2011*). That's a lot of teenagers taking a lot of uncalculated risks and, whilst research points towards factors such as social deprivation and disadvantage, every teen is vulnerable and it only takes one lapse of judgement for conception to occur.

Contraception

Contraception is a pill, injection or device that is used to stop a woman getting pregnant. There are many options available and it can become confusing. Certain contraceptives can only be used by women of a certain age, whilst others can't be used if the woman has certain existing health conditions. If you don't know the pros and cons of each option, or you're not aware of all the options available, then your teen can discuss these with a nurse.

Not just pregnancy

Whilst most contraceptives will prevent pregnancy occurring in the majority of cases (none are 100% effective), your teen should be aware that they won't protect them against STIs. The only way to prevent the transmission of STIs is to wear a condom. If you only teach your teen one fact about sex, teach them this. If you know your teen is sexually active, or is likely to experiment in the near future, buy them some condoms, or take them to a sexual health clinic. They might be too embarrassed to buy or ask for them themselves, although switched-on teens are less inhibited about this than in years gone by, and condoms are more readily available to teenagers these days.

What are the choices?

Whilst your son or daughter should always have a packet of condoms close to hand, your sexually active daughter should also take other contraceptive precautions. After all, condoms split, and teens can make spontaneous decisions in the heat of the moment.

Caps and diaphragms

These fit over the cervix and stop pregnancy, as the sperm can't reach the egg. You need to use them each time you have sex, and they have to be used with spermicide. They are slightly less effective than other forms of contraception.

Combined pill (the pill)

The pill contains two female hormones that occur naturally in the ovaries. The pill stops an egg from being released each month, so the woman can't get pregnant. There are different types of pill – your teen's doctor will advise which is the best for them to take. The pill is taken each day for a cycle of 21 days a month and it's over 99% effective against pregnancy. For more information see *The Pill – The Essential Guide*, Need2Know.

Condom

Although female condoms are available, it's the male condom that's the contraceptive of choice. It's small, easy to carry, and easy to put on. Some men say that it inhibits sexual pleasure but modern condoms offer little in the way of a barrier. The condom is the only contraceptive that prevents the spread of STIs.

Contraceptive injection

There are two types available – one lasts for two months and one lasts for three months. The injection contains the hormone progestogen and it stops the ovaries releasing an egg each month. It is over 99% effective.

Contraceptive implant

This is a thin tube that is put under the skin, where it releases the hormone progestogen over a period of three years. It can be removed at any time but it's over 99% effective when it's in place.

Emergency contraception

This is a pill that is taken orally, up to 72 hours after having unprotected sex. It works by stopping the fertilisation of an egg, and the sooner you take it after having sex, the more effective it will be. You can also use an IUD as emergency contraception. It works in the same way and can be fitted up to five days after having unprotected sex.

Intrauterine device (IUD)

This small plastic and copper device is placed in the womb, where it can stay for up to ten years, offering 99% effectiveness against pregnancy. The copper in the device is a spermicide and this is gradually released over time.

Intrauterine system (IUS)

This is similar to the IUD but, instead of releasing copper, it releases the hormone progestogen. It lasts for up to five years, and is up to 99% effective.

Progestogen-only pill (POP)

This contraceptive pill only contains one hormone – progestogen – and it's used by women who can't take the pill, for whatever reason. You take this contraceptive every day.

STIs

No one knows for sure who their sexual partners have previously slept with, and whether or not their previous partners have been carrying an STI. Many STIs can remain dormant for months – or the symptoms at least are undetectable – which means that you can't tell just by looking at someone if they're infected. This reiterates the importance of wearing a condom for every sexual encounter, as this is the only way to fully protect yourself against getting an STI.

If your teen is worried that they might have been exposed to an STI, it's important to get it checked out immediately. You can make an appointment with your doctor, or visit an NHS GUM (genitourinary medicine) clinic, or sexual health clinic, to get tested. There's more information below about different STIs.

Chlamydia

This can go undetected for a long time. If you do have symptoms, they could include bleeding, discomfort when you go to the toilet, or discharge. A simple test will let you know if you're infected and it is treated with antibiotics.

'No one knows for sure who their sexual partners have previously slept with, and whether or not their previous partners have been carrying an STI.'

Genital herpes

This infection will lie dormant most of the time, but you might get regular outbreaks of blisters around the genital area.

Genital warts

This unpleasant-sounding infection consists of small lumps on the skin around the genital area. It's usually treated with cream.

Gonorrhoea

If this gets left undiagnosed, it can eventually lead to infertility. You'll notice discharge from your vagina or penis and you may experience discomfort when you urinate. It is treated with antibiotics.

HIV

This virus attacks your immune system and can eventually lead to AIDS. HIV can be controlled with treatment but there's no cure for the virus.

Pubic lice

These are tiny insects that live in hair, and they particularly like pubic hair. You'll notice itching around the genital area and insecticide is used to treat it.

Scabies

This is caused by minute mites that dig under the skin and cause itching. It's treated with insecticide.

Syphilis

This Dickensian-sounding infection is very infectious. It produces sores on the genitals, which appear and disappear over a period of weeks. The symptoms continue and it can be a serious illness if it's not treated, leading to major long-term health issues like blindness.

Trichomoniasis

This parasite causes itching and discomfort. It is treated with antibiotics.

The law on sex

The law on the age of consent varies slightly around the UK. The age of consent for men and women in all countries (England, Wales, Scotland and Northern Ireland) is 16. However, in England and Wales, there is some leeway with regards to sexual activity with consent between two people of a younger age, as long as no abuse or exploitation was involved. Whereas, in Scotland, sexual intercourse between young people of 13 to 15 remains a criminal offence, even if both parties consented. In all countries, there are specific laws in place to protect children under the age of 13, as they cannot legally give their consent.

There are obviously certain situations where the law can become a bit blurred, but teens need to be extremely careful, as the excuse that someone looked older will not necessarily be accepted.

'The law on the age of consent varies slightly around the UK.'

Age of consent between same-sex partners

The age of consent between men, and between women, is also 16; and the same laws apply to sexual activity between men, and between women, as to heterosexual sex.

A–Z of sex

Whether it's you or your teen that needs the low-down on sexual terms, you can find out more in this quick guide.

Abortion
The termination of a pregnancy. UK law states that a woman can have an abortion up to the twenty-fourth week of her pregnancy, with the type of abortion being dependant upon the stage of the pregnancy. For more information take a look at *Abortion – The Essential Guide*, published by Need2Know.

Age of consent
This is the age the law says you can legally have sexual intercourse. In the UK, it's 16.

AIDS (Acquired immune deficiency syndrome)
A condition that attacks the body's immune system. It's caused by the virus HIV, which can be sexually transmitted.

Anal sex
Sexual intercourse in the anus.

Birth control
This can refer to any type of contraception that prevents pregnancy.

Bisexual
A person who is attracted to both men and women.

Blow job
Using your mouth on the penis for sexual arousal.

Cap
A type of contraceptive that fits over a woman's cervix to stop the sperm from reaching the egg.

Celibacy
Abstaining from sexual intercourse.

Cervical smear
A test where cells are extracted from the cervix using a speculum and tested to check a woman for cervical cancer.

Cervix
This is the lower end of the uterus and it connects the womb to the vagina.

Chlamydia
A sexually transmitted disease that can lead to infertility in women.

Circumcision
A minor operation to remove the foreskin from the penis. Men might be circumcised for religious or health reasons.

Clitoris
A small, sensitive area above the opening of the vagina. It is only found in females and its primary function is to create sexual pleasure.

Combined pill
A type of contraceptive that is taken by a woman once a day.

Condom
Most common contraceptive for protection against unwanted pregnancy and sexually transmitted infections.

Contraception
Any preventative measures used or taken, to stop a woman getting pregnant. Examples include the pill and condoms.

Date rape
Forced sexual intercourse that occurs on a date.

Depo-Provera
Form of contraceptive where a woman has an injection once every three months.

Diaphragm
(see cap)

Dildo
Penis-shaped sex toy used for sexual pleasure.

Ectopic pregnancy
When an egg is fertilised outside of the womb. The pregnancy is dangerous for the mother and baby and will generally result in a termination.

Emergency pill
Contraceptive pill that can be taken up to three days after sexual intercourse.

Ejaculation
When a man climaxes during sexual activity, sperm is released from his penis.

Erection
When a man's penis becomes enlarged and hard when he is aroused, and he is then ready to have intercourse.

Fallopian tubes
These attach the ovaries to the womb.

Family planning
Advice on all aspects of sex, contraception, pregnancy and STIs.

Foreplay
The sexual activity that leads up to penetrative sex.

Foreskin
The layer of skin that covers the top of the penis.

Gay
Being sexually attracted to people of the same sex. Another word for homosexual.

Gender identity disorder
When you feel unsure about whether you are the gender that you were assigned at birth.

Genitals
The reproductive organs of a man or woman.

Genital warts
An STI with symptoms of raised lumps on the genital area.

Gonorrhoea
This is an STI that is treated with antibiotics.

GUM clinic (genitourinary medicine)
Sexual health clinics that are run by the NHS.

Hard-on
Another name for an erect penis.

Hepatitis
A liver disease that can be contracted through sexual intercourse.

Heterosexual
When you're sexually attracted to someone of the opposite sex.

HIV
A virus that can be sexually transmitted and can progress to AIDS.

Homosexual
Another word for gay, or when you're attracted to someone of the same sex.

Hormones
Chemicals that result in puberty and the changes in the body that signify adulthood.

Hymen
A layer of skin over the vagina. If it is still intact when you first have sex, it can be uncomfortable or painful when it breaks.

Impotence
If a man can't get or maintain an erection.

IUD
A type of contraceptive.

Labia
The two layers of skin that surround and protect the clitoris and the openings of the vagina and urethra. The outer labia are known as labia majora, and the inner layer, the labia minora.

Lesbian
A woman who is attracted to other women.

Love bites
If you suck your partner's skin, it can leave red bruise-like marks. Also known as hickeys.

Lubricant
Cream or liquid that is applied to the vagina or penis to make sex easier and more enjoyable.

Masturbation
To bring yourself or your partner to orgasm by pleasuring the vagina or penis.

Menstrual cycle
A woman's cycle starts when she begins her period. All women have different cycles, but they're generally just under a month in length.

Miscarriage
When a pregnancy ends before the baby can survive outside of the womb.

Morning-after pill
Emergency contraceptive taken after having unprotected sex.

Oral sex
Using your mouth to give oral pleasure to your partner's genitals.

Orgasm
An intense rush of pleasure when sexual climax is achieved.

Ovulation
A woman's ovaries release an egg about halfway through her monthly cycle. If this egg is fertilised she can become pregnant.

Perineum
This is the area between the vagina or scrotum, and the anus.

Period
Another word for menstruation – when a woman has her monthly bleed.

Pornography
Sexually explicit images or films.

Premature ejaculation
When a man ejaculates very soon into sexual intercourse. It's very common when men first have sex.

Puberty
Physical changes that occur when a child becomes an adult.

Pubic hair
Hair that grows around the genital area.

Rape
When a person is forced into having sex without their consent.

Rimming
Using your tongue to provide sexual pleasure to your partner's anus.

Safer sex
Using adequate protection when having sex. This means protecting yourself against STIs, as well as unwanted pregnancy.

Semen
The liquid that comes out of a man's penis when he ejaculates.

Sexual intercourse
Vaginal or anal sex between heterosexual or homosexual partners.

Sexuality
This is used to refer to whether a person is heterosexual, homosexual or bisexual.

Smear test

Women over the age of 25 should have regular smear tests to check for signs of cervical cancer. (See cervical smear.)

Sperm

Another word for semen. The liquid that comes out of a man's penis when he ejaculates.

STI

Sexually transmitted infection.

Tampons

These are used by girls when they are having a period. They are inserted into the vagina to absorb the blood. They're painless to use.

Testicles

Also known as 'balls', these produce sperm and are protected by the scrotum.

Thrush

An uncomfortable condition that causes itching.

Transsexual

Someone who wants to live as the opposite sex to that which they have been born. Some people choose to have gender reassignment surgery, where the physical appearance and function of their existing sexual organs/ characteristics are surgically altered to become those of the other sex.

Transvestite

A man or woman who dresses as a member of the opposite sex (so a man dressing as a woman, or a woman dressing as a man).

Unprotected sex

Having sexual intercourse without using contraception.

Vagina

A woman's genitals, protected by two sets of labia – or lips.

Virgin

Someone who has not engaged in sexual activity – generally referring to penetration.

Vulva

The external part of the woman's genitals that encompasses the openings of the vagina and urethra, the labia and the clitoris.

Wet dreams

This usually refers to a man ejaculating in his sleep but it can happen to women too.

Summing Up

- Be prepared for puberty and make sure your child knows exactly what changes are going to occur.

- Try to be understanding about mood swings and slammed doors: this is a trying time for everyone, especially your teen.

- Talk to your teen as an equal: if they're old enough to be having sex, they're old enough to hear some home truths and hard-hitting facts about pregnancy and STIs.

- Make sure you and your teen know about all the contraception options available to them. Remember, condoms are the only contraceptives that protect against STIs as well as unwanted pregnancies.

- Remind your teen about the law – the age of consent is in place for a reason.

Chapter Five

The Emotional Side of Sex

Peer pressure

Children want to fit in with their friends, and this becomes more apparent as they get older. They don't want to be seen as the odd one out for any reason and, unfortunately, this can extend to sexual behaviour. Much playground banter is exaggerated or completely made up, but once kids become sexually active, there's a certain amount of peer pressure to do what everyone else is doing. Whether or not they're actually doing it is largely irrelevant and bragging about sex is commonplace amongst teens.

Confidence is key

If you have regular conversations with your kids about sex and relationships, they will have the confidence that comes with knowledge and the ability to make their own decisions based on facts and emotional maturity, rather than hearsay. They can stand up for their own principles and look at things from different perspectives. When they can see both sides of the argument, they'll soon realise that most of what they hear in the playground should be taken with a pinch of salt. With this realisation comes power: the confidence to question, the authority to say 'no' and the strength to ignore the pressure or the jibes. Being a bit streetwise means your teen won't be seen as a walkover.

'Children want to fit in with their friends, and this becomes more apparent as they get older.'

Relationship life skills

Your child's first impressions of relationships will be gleaned from you. Whether you're in a heterosexual or same-sex partnership or marriage, or you're a single parent, the way you conduct your relationships will act as a kind of template for your kids. Obviously, as they grow up and mature and embark on their own relationships, they'll start to make their own judgements and impart their own values into their ideas about relationships, but essentially, you will form the building blocks of their knowledge from a very early age.

Mutual respect

Relationships are a vital part of life, and we're not just talking about sexual relationships. The way you act with your friends, the way you talk to your children, your social conduct and your values and attitudes will all have an input into their psyche. Before they have the life experience to weigh up arguments and make their own judgements, kids will take their cues from you and this is how they build up their database of values. It might sound petty, but if they see you drop litter or hear you use derogatory terms, they'll think it's acceptable to do the same. And why wouldn't they? When kids are young, you're the axle that their limited world spins around.

Set an example

And so it is with life partners. If your kids see you and your partner in a mutually respectful relationship, this will be the norm: the benchmark with which they measure their own – or other people's – relationships. If, however, they see power play, constant arguments, a lack of respect, or an uneven division of work and responsibilities between you and your partner, their view of relationships will be very different.

Do the right thing checklist

- Try not to let arguments escalate in front of your kids.
- Emphasise the importance of gender equality through your own actions.

Need2Know

- Tell your kids you love them and don't be afraid to show your emotions.

- Whatever the dynamics of your family unit, make it clear that you're a team – in it together and always there for each other.

- Live by your own advice: teach your kids to respect other people, to be open-minded and accepting and to expect the same treatment in return.

How does your teen know they're ready for sex?

If you ask any adult whether they felt they were ready for their first sexual encounter, you'd probably get an overwhelming number reflecting that they probably weren't. Hindsight is a wonderful thing but the trouble is, teenagers are too young to have the benefit of hindsight to steer them onwards in life, especially when it comes to relationships. They're chartering brand new territory, and they have no personal experience on which to base their decisions and behaviour. So, teenagers often feel that they're ready to have sex; that they have the maturity to deal with it; and their bodies are telling them they're ready, when perhaps they're not.

Confusing sexual desire with love

They've seen it on the telly, they've heard their friends talking about it and they've met someone they want to have sex with. But is that enough? For many teens, sex and love are mutually exclusive, especially when it comes to getting sexual experience and giving into the urges of rampant hormones. Puberty brings with it huge waves of emotions, and physical attraction is a big part of this. Sex can be a series of successful, or unsuccessful, experiments at that age, whereas love, respect and the nature of meaningful relationships are issues that need to be learned, developed and explored with more care.

'Hindsight is a wonderful thing but the trouble is, teenagers are too young to have the benefit of hindsight to steer them onwards in life.'

The easy option

Lust and love are intertwined and often confused; peer pressure is rife and virginity can seem like annoying extra baggage that teens want to shift as quickly as possible. Sometimes, saying 'yes' can be much easier than saying 'no' and there can be extra pressure from a partner who declares their undying love and insists that sex is the next step in the relationship.

Time to talk

It can be difficult to explain the differences between sexual desire and emotional love to your teen. They might be desperate to just get their first time out of the way and therefore not in a good place to take on board any of your advice. No matter, you can try to talk to them anyway, put across your side of the argument and ask them to really think about their actions.

If you're lucky, they'll come to you first to talk about it; if not, try and pre-empt the conversation and go to them. At the end of the day, you can't dissuade or stop them but you should ask the questions that they should be asking themselves to ensure that it's the right thing to do. Don't go overboard – you don't want to come across as a nagging parent – they'll make their own decisions in the end and they'll learn by their own mistakes, as you did when you were their age. The most important thing is to make sure that your teen isn't facing pressure to do anything they don't want to do, or don't feel ready for yet.

'As a parent, it's extremely difficult to advise your teen to wait when everything in their being is telling them they should have sex.'

How to say no to sex even in the face of love

If your son or daughter really is experiencing the first flush of young love, it's very tricky to make the distinction between emotional and physical attraction. They may feel like they have to have sex with their partner to avoid being dumped, or they may genuinely feel ready to take that next step.

As a parent, it's extremely difficult to advise your teen to wait when everything in their being is telling them they should have sex. You don't want to belittle their relationship or to confuse what you're telling them by saying that sex is out of the question whatever the situation. All you can really do is to ask them to really question their relationship:

- Would their partner dump them if they refused to have sex?

- Would it be better to wait a while longer to make sure the relationship is a lasting one?

- Has their partner slept with lots of other people already? If so, are they really looking for a relationship, or just another sexual encounter?

- Is this the person your son or daughter wants to give their virginity away to?

If they can answer questions like this with clarity and honesty then you have done all you can in your capacity as a carer, with the best interests of your child as your sole concern. If they choose to have sex, you should give them all the advice about contraception, conception, STIs and other family planning issues and respect their right to make their own decision.

Building self-esteem

The more confidence and self awareness your teen has, the less likely they are to be pressurised into sex, or to fall into sexual relationships on the promise of something more meaningful. Knowledge is key but it needs to be combined with a sense of self-esteem. If you feel worthless, you naturally crave attention, and love – in any guise – can seem like the great escape. It's easy for confusion to arise as to whether someone is giving you attention through romantic love or just through sexual attention and, if your teen has low self-esteem they might not be able to differentiate between the two.

You can help to build up your kids' confidence and to develop their sense of self-worth and their place in the world. If they learn to value love and friendship and to demand respect in all of their relationships, they are less likely to engage in sexual activity for the wrong reasons. The problem is that meaningless sex, and the realisation that they've been used simply for sexual gratification, will ultimately lead to greater self-doubt and the cycle could continue.

Sex should be special

Try to make them aware that sex with the right person is an all-encompassing experience that should affect you on both an emotional and a physical level. It's not just about instant gratification; it's about learning more about each other on a very personal level and developing a deep physical bond with someone. This takes time and understanding and sexual gratification is by no means guaranteed with every experience. Unfulfilling sexual encounters can be very disappointing – a severe anticlimax for a teen who has seen a thousand on-screen orgasms, or relationships as seen through the rose-tinted spectacles of the romantic comedy.

Peer pressure checklist

- Look out for signs such as your teen becoming introverted or especially moody and sullen.

- Try to engage them in conversation, even if they say they don't want to talk, remind them you're there whenever they're ready, and they can tell you anything.

- Be wary of new partners or new friends who elicit changes to your teen's personality.

- Encourage your teen to see other friends, engage in other activities and to be their own person, with their own opinions.

- Talk to them about the importance of being ready for sex, or not feeling pressurised and of being with a partner who feels mutual affection and pleasure is important.

- There's no hurry – they have the rest of their life to discover and develop sexual relationships.

Sexual identity and being gay

Many parents will know well before puberty if their son or daughter is gay. They'll pick up on the signs from a very early age, or they'll have the conversation with their child, when they're ready to tell them. Sexual orientation is no longer the stuff of whispered conversations for most people – it's a fact of life. Kids are more clued up and, although bullying still occurs, things are better at school for gay children who choose to 'come out' to their peers. That's not to brush aside the very real and ongoing issues of homophobia and prejudice, but society is generally a more accepting place and, with each generation of kids, the myths are dispelled a little more and people are less 'shocked'.

The first you heard

However, if you have no idea that your child is gay, then their coming out could be a genuine shock. Some parents feel upset, overwhelmed, maybe even embarrassed about what their friends will say. Most will have apprehensions about their child growing up gay in a society that still has pockets of homophobia. Your reaction to the news will really depend on your own exposure to gay culture. If you have gay friends then you will probably have a great deal more awareness of the issues faced by gay people, and a greater propensity to accept the information more easily and calmly. If, however, your gay knowledge only extends as far as celebrities and issues of sexual health, you've got a lot to learn.

Don't distance yourself

Whatever you do, and however shocked you might feel on initially discovering that your son or daughter is gay, don't shy away from the situation. Talk to them about it; be honest about your feelings and express your concerns. It takes a lot of courage to come out so respect the journey that your child has gone through to reach this point and talk to them about it.

It's just a phase

If your child has made the momentous decision to tell you about his or her sexuality, chances are it's not 'just a phase'. This is usually a myth that concerned parents create to try and rationalise the situation – to brush it aside as a simple case of hormones or teenage angst. However, by treating it as such, you're trivialising the identity of your child, pretending that they're something they're not, and belittling their decision to tell you. Don't be afraid to tell your child that you're finding it tough to take it all in: honesty is good, ignoring the

'Whatever you do, and however shocked you might feel on initially discovering that your son or daughter is gay, don't shy away from the situation.'

situation is unhelpful for everyone. If you want some independent support, there are many charities and groups that help young gay people and their parents or carers, such as FFLAG (Families and Friends of Lesbians and Gays). See the help list at the back of the book for contact details.

Summing Up

* Teens can be very vulnerable to peer pressure. Try and give them the confidence and skills to speak their mind, go against the crowd and say 'no'.

* Talk to your teen about the emotional side of sex – encourage them to question their own readiness.

* It's easy to confuse lust with love and to rush into a sexual relationship: try to help them understand the difference.

* If you son or daughter 'comes out' as being gay, offer support and help them work through issues such as bullying or isolation.

Chapter Six

Different Strokes for Different Folks

Which parent should do the talking?

When you were a child, you might remember being sat down with your mum (if you're female), or your dad (if you're male) for 'the chat'. It was probably a fairly staid and formal situation, where the basics of menstruation, puberty, sex and reproduction were imparted to you in one sitting. Depending on your age and experience, you were probably left very confused, or unenlightened by this – either the bombardment of information made your head swim, or you had already gleaned the information from other sources.

Obviously, not all households were the same and you might have had liberal parents who spoke openly about sex issues, as and when they arose. However, for most parents, it was probably a one-off conversation with much awkwardness and embarrassment on both sides.

'Kids and parents are more enlightened these days.'

Moving on

Luckily, times have changed. Kids and parents are more enlightened these days. Parents have a better grip on what the younger generation get up to, and kids are more willing to ask the questions that are bothering them. That's not to say that both parties are happy to chat about menstrual cycles over breakfast cereal but things have definitely moved on. And, it's the same when it comes to who does the talking.

No set rules

If both parents are present in the household, there are no hard and fast rules that state Dad should be dealing with the boys and Mum with the girls. Two parents simply means two points of view, and this is great news for curious kids. If you really want to create an atmosphere of openness and honesty when it comes to talking about sex with your kids, then you need to make it clear that both parents are available to talk about anything at any time. It's important for girls to have a male perspective about sex and relationships, and likewise for a boy to know what it's like from a woman's point of view. If we're teaching our kids that sex isn't a taboo subject in the home then we need to follow through by ensuring everyone is happy to do the talking.

The exceptions

Obviously, a male or female perspective is helpful for certain aspects of puberty and sex and your kids might naturally gravitate towards one parent for certain gaps in their knowledge. For example, Dad obviously won't be able to offer any first-hand experience of menstruation and Mum will only be able to speak objectively to her son about wet dreams and male masturbation. That's not to say that kids have to talk exclusively to Mum or Dad about certain things – they just might want to get both sides of the story and talk to someone with the necessary experience.

What if you're a single parent?

If you're a single parent, you're probably used to covering all bases with your kids. You're 'good cop' and 'bad cop', you're the provider, the home-maker, the disciplinarian and the shoulder to cry on – all the time. Every parent knows that it's both extremely tough, and extremely rewarding to bring up kids and, if you're doing it on your own, you make all the decisions. When it comes to discussing sex and relationships, your child will obviously just have one parent around all the time who they can confide in and the information they receive will be from a purely male or female perspective. However, there's no reason for kids of single parents to have any less of a grounding in sex and relationship issues, than kids from a two-parent household.

Boys and girls

If you're a woman with sons, then you might need to do a little extra homework on specifically male issues and likewise, if you're a single dad with girls. But, at the end of the day, kids just want the information – if they're confident and used to an open environment when it comes to talking, then it really doesn't matter who that information comes from.

Role models

Some single parents seek help from close friends or relatives when it comes to talking about specific sex topics. Perhaps your kids feel embarrassed about discussing certain things with you, or maybe you feel that your son or daughter could benefit from having a chat to someone of the same gender, just to fill in any gaps in their knowledge. If your kids have godparents or aunts and uncles who they're close to, you could ask if they'd be willing to chat to them. This doesn't have to be a formal sit-down chat; it should just be spontaneous conversations, perhaps sparked by the adult in a natural way.

What you need to know about boy worries and girl worries

When you talk to your kids, try to think about things from their perspective and to pre-empt some of the more tricky questions they might have, or the things that might worry them. There's a fine line between teaching them about the dangers and leaving them anxious or confused, and it's difficult to get the balance right.

'When you talk to your kids, try to think about things from their perspective and to pre-empt some of the more tricky questions they might have.'

Gender-specific worries

You should be aware of the different things that boys and girls worry about. For example, they might have fears about contracting specific STIs; girls might have concerns about getting pregnant, or boys about getting someone pregnant. There could be anxiety about what to do when things get intimate with a partner, or girls might have issues about saying 'no', taking things further, or how to insist that a partner wears a condom.

The information you take for granted hasn't all necessarily filtered down to your kids and it only takes a small information gap, or a confused message to send them into spasms of worry. Obviously, you don't want to pry too deeply into your kids' personal lives – and there does need to be a cut-off point between concerned parent and intrusive parent. You don't need to know the intimate details of your kids' relationships, and they won't want to discuss this with you but you should be open to talking about whatever they want to.

'The information you take for granted hasn't all necessarily filtered down to your kids and it only takes a small information gap, or a confused message to send them into spasms of worry.'

Typical boy worries:

- Is my penis the right shape/size?

- Will I know what to do the first time I have sex?

- I want to sleep with my girlfriend but she says she's not ready.

- Will it hurt my girlfriend if she is a virgin?

- Will she tell all her friends if I don't do it right?

Typical girl worries:

- Why haven't I had my first period yet?

- How do I know if I'm ready to have sex?

- Will it hurt the first time I have sex?

- I think I might be pregnant.

- How can I say 'no' when a boy is trying to persuade me to sleep with him?

Gender peer pressure and how to cope with it

We've talked about peer pressure already (see chapter 5) but it's worth mentioning again in the context of talking to your kids. This can be a constant worry and kids need to have strength of will to stand out from their friends. It's easy to see how kids feel pressurised into having sex before they feel ready, if only to avoid the jibes, or to be part of 'the club'. If all their friends spend their free time discussing boyfriends or girlfriends, it's tough to stand around on the sidelines as the odd one out.

You need to constantly reassure your teen that losing their virginity isn't about scoring points or winning a race. They should wait until they feel ready to take such a big step, with the right person. Remind them that teens tend to talk the talk but they don't always walk the walk – many of their friends will be exaggerating about what they've done, and almost certainly exaggerating about how great it was. First encounters can be overrated, especially if the sex is casual and meaningless and not in the context of a mutually caring relationship.

Boys and girls and STIs

Boys and girls will naturally have different concerns about STIs, as different conditions can affect the sexes in different ways. Serious STIs such as gonorrhoea and chlamydia can have very few obvious symptoms early on, which makes it even more important for men to wear a condom, even if the woman is taking another form of birth control.

If your teen is concerned that they might have an STI – perhaps they had a sexual encounter with someone they have since discovered has an infection, or they have some symptoms – then it's important to get them checked out immediately. Most STIs can be treated quickly once they are diagnosed but, the longer they're left, the more serious the side effects can become.

How boys and girls handle sex

Sex can prompt a number of emotional responses, and girls and boys will handle it in very different ways. The stereotype of the girl falling in love and the boy falling in lust does have some truth, especially when it comes to dealing with rampant teenage hormones. Generally, girls talk to each other more, and about more intimate topics, as well as those relating to their emotional feelings about sex and relationships. They're more likely to dissect a relationship – or potential relationship – to second-guess the feelings of the boy in question, and to want more emotional attachment from their partner.

Boy talk

Girls tend to mature before boys, so boys will suddenly find themselves in an adult body with adult feelings and sexual desires, but they might not be quite ready to deal with the associated emotional side of a relationship. For boys, there are also the unwritten rules of bravado, which mean they're less likely to discuss their feelings, sticking more to the bare facts of the situation. As parents, you might find it easier to get information from your daughter than your son. That doesn't mean your son doesn't necessarily want to talk to you (although this might be the case!); it's just that girls tend to show their emotions more than boys, and are more open to talking about their relationships, crushes and heartaches.

Double standards and name-calling

When it comes to sexual behaviour, there is still an incredibly one-sided attitude amongst teens about male and female sexual activity. Although times have changed, people have more liberated views and sexual activity is discussed more openly in the home, when it comes to actually having sex, boys and girls are viewed very differently by each other, their peers and, unfortunately, by the world at large.

Boys will be boys

If a boy is sexually active and has a number of sexual partners, it's seen as something to brag about, almost like a rite of passage on his route to becoming a man. However, when a girl acts in the same way, she is seen as being 'loose', she gets a bad reputation and inevitably, she ends up being talked about by the boys, the girls and the parents.

Bullying

Kids can be cruel and they will tease and bully each other for not having sex, for being gay or for sleeping around and therefore being labelled 'loose'. Talk to your teen about bullying and the importance of trying to stay strong and sticking to your principles. If they are being bullied, try and keep a close eye on the situation and talk to the school. Not all kids are confident enough to stand up to bullies, or to take the taunts with a pinch of salt. You want them to make their own informed decisions and not to have their actions determined by pressure or bullying from their peers.

When kids reach their teens, bullying more often involves sexual slander or even harassment from the opposite sex. Girls become jealous of other girls, boys might vie for the attention of a particular girl, or lose face if a girl won't date them or have sex with them. The original reason for a bout of bullying might not even be that clear, but things can escalate quickly and it doesn't take long for one child to become ostracised, as others join the bandwagon. Bullying can have long-term psychological effects on a child so it needs to be tackled from the outset. If you need extra help and support, you can contact groups like Kidscape or Family Lives (see the help list), or take a look at Jennifer Thomson's book *Bullying – A Parent's Guide*, Need2Know.

Summing Up

- Make it clear to your kids that both parents are happy to talk to them about sex and relationships.

- Single parents can supply all the information their kids need.

- Some people might ask close friends or relatives to help out with tricky topics.

- Be aware that your kids don't necessarily know everything – they could be worried about something that might seem trivial to you.

- Boys and girls will have different concerns and will want to talk to you about different things and to a different degree.

- Be aware of gender-specific behaviour when it comes to teen relationships.

Chapter Seven

The Truth About Love

The media view of love

Teens today are bombarded with mixed messages about love and relationships, and this can only add to their confusion when they're trying to figure out their own sexual identity, values and feelings about each other. With Hollywood films packed with happy ever afters, supermodel couples and endless romantic gestures and orgasms, it's little wonder that teens feel let down by their first experiences of sex and relationships.

Hollywood romance

Teenage girls might expect to be whisked away on romantic breaks, treated to romantic meals and have the car door opened for them and flowers presented at the start of every date. However, fried chicken and an awkward fumble in the back of the cinema soon put paid to their lofty romantic dreams and they learn to adjust their expectations. That's not to say that teen relationships are a let-down; nothing quite beats the excitement of a first date or a first kiss. It's just a lot of relationships have a gaping gap between the fictional expectations and the down-to-earth reality of real relationships.

Reality check

Genuine, loving relationships are few and far between, but teens are often desperate to discover those feelings. So much so that they'll confuse a crush with love, stumbling through their first couple of relationships as they find their feet and begin to learn what it is they expect from a partner and the levels of give and take they're prepared to accept.

'Teens today are bombarded with mixed messages about love and relationships.'

What is love and what does it mean?

Real love involves total commitment to a relationship. It also involves sacrifice, honesty, openness, affection and a genuine physical and emotional bond. Having just gone through puberty, and a whirlwind of hormonal changes, these are not attributes that many teens possess. It's not unheard of; it's just not common. Teen love will be based on their experience thus far: celebrity crushes; bonds of friendship; and the love of a solid family unit. They won't have experienced genuine romantic love or the sheer rush of emotions that comes with it.

Playing the field

Teens are exploring their own bodies, exploring each other's bodies, and generally discovering themselves and evolving into independent adults. It's only natural that they won't really have a firm hold of the future; of where they want it to take them or what they want to do. So it's hardly surprising that not many of them are planning a future with a partner at this stage in their lives. In fact, it can be difficult for teens to hold down serious relationships, as they're often not taken seriously, and their friends will be busy flitting between boyfriends and girlfriends.

Being in a teen relationship

Different kids – boys and girls – can have very different views about what a relationship actually involves. Whilst innocent hand-holding and walking home together after school might constitute an exclusive dating relationship for one person, the other could be walking home – or doing a whole lot more – with someone different every night. When you're exploring the boundaries, you have no idea what to expect, or what other people expect, so it's a massive learning curve and there are bound to be heartaches along the way.

That's not to say that teens aren't capable of having meaningful relationships. No one knows how or when they're going to meet 'the right person' so who is to say it won't be when you're a teenager. Let's face it: if you can weather the storm of puberty, hormones, teenage angst and the pressure to sleep around, then it's actually a pretty good basis for a long-term relationship.

Not quite an adult

It can be difficult to set the boundaries for teen relationships. Whilst your son or daughter might be seriously involved with a partner, and you might be aware that they are sleeping with each other, they're not quite an adult. They still live at home; they don't have independent means and are not likely to in the near future. That means you still set the rules and the boundaries. They might feel as if they should be treated as adults – as they are essentially conducting an adult relationship – and yet you still pay their mobile phone bill and give them an allowance.

It's tricky for both parties to get the balance right. If you know the relationship is serious, it's appropriate to respect that. That doesn't necessarily mean you have to allow their partner to stay over, but you should respect their right to privacy to a certain extent.

Peer pressure and self-esteem

We've talked about the pressures to have sex, and to have sex with lots of people. Teens face intense pressure from their peers in all aspects of their lives but especially when it comes to sex. Having sex is often a far easier option than holding on to their virginity and justifying their decision to abstain. Sex means attention – from the partner and from their peers – and this can be attractive to teens who suffer from low self-esteem, or other confidence issues. They may mistake sexual attention for genuine love and this can be a tricky cycle to break. Sex can be used as a substitute for a lack of attention or affection elsewhere in their lives.

If you think your teen might be sleeping around due to peer pressure or to get attention, you need to address the problem immediately. Talk to them to find out if they're being bullied, of if they're being sexually harassed or intimidated. There could be more deep-rooted issues, in which case you should seek counselling for your teen.

'It can be difficult to set the boundaries for teen relationships.'

Knowing when to have sex

Is there ever a right time for the first time? It's a tough question for inquisitive teens with sexual urges, but the fact they're asking the questions means that they're thinking about it, rather than simply rushing in. If your teen comes to you for advice, you should count yourself lucky that you have such an open and trusting relationship with them.

Your initial reaction will probably be to tell them they should wait; that they're too young to cope with the emotional side of sex; and that they should hold out until they've met someone they envisage spending their life with. However, you also need to be realistic and, much as this advice is good advice, you should also offer your teen help for the situation in hand, and talk them through the scenario of the here and now. If you merely talk the situation away until some time in the distant future, you're not going to help prepare them for the practicalities of sex, and you're making the assumption that they will follow your advice to the letter, even if they want to act otherwise.

Ask the questions

With the benefit of experience, you're in an ideal situation to help and advise your teen. You might not want to be too specific, or go into too many personal details, but you can get them to think about how they feel about having sex, how they might feel afterwards, as well as telling them that expectations and reality can be far apart. Once they've lost their virginity, there's no going back so it's important to be ready.

How will I know if I'm ready? checklist

- Are you making the decision to have sex of your own accord, or do you feel pressurised by your partner?

- Do you trust your partner and know them well?

- Are you confident that they don't have a reputation for playing the field, or are likely to have an STI?

- Are you aware of the precautions you need to take, and are you using contraception?

- Do you love and respect your partner, and does he or she feel the same about you?

Being single and coping with it

Teenagers tend to flit between relationships as they work out what they want, what works, what they'll accept and what behaviour is a deal-breaker. However, there may come a time when your teen's friends are all happily strolling along hand in hand with boyfriends or girlfriends and ducking out of nights out with their mates to go on dates instead. Your teen might feel like the only single kid on the block, and this can be an isolating experience. They probably feel like everyone else is getting on with the business of sex and relationships, while they're being left in the dark and on the shelf.

Stay active

If your teen has 'lost' their friends to relationships, encourage them to get out and meet new people. If they're interested in sport they could join a new club, or take up a new hobby. It's not just about hooking up with someone for a relationship; it's about boosting their confidence and stopping them moping around the house feeling sorry for themselves. They're more likely to meet a girlfriend or boyfriend if they're happy, outgoing and have something to talk about. Chances are, a lot of their attached friends will be single again further down the line, and they'll be nagging your teen to go out with them.

'Teenagers tend to flit between relationships as they work out what they want, what works, what they'll accept and what behaviour is a deal-breaker.'

Summing Up

- Many teens will have a distorted view of love, generated by the media.

- Be around to console and reassure when those first few relationships don't pan out like a Hollywood film.

- Talk to your teen about the commitment, mutual respect, trust and honesty that are part and parcel of genuine, loving relationships.

- Respect your teen's relationship – they are no less meaningful to them, just because they're young and inexperienced.

- Seek help and advice if you think your teen is actively seeking sexual attention as a result of peer pressure or self-esteem issues.

- They need to learn to be happy being single and not to rely on relationships, or constantly strive to be in one.

Chapter Eight

Techniques for the Super-Embarrassed Parent

How to overcome embarrassment about sex

Everyone gets embarrassed when talking about sex. And, if you happen to be talking to your own kids, the embarrassment on both sides is likely to be even more acute. Although kids really want to talk to you, it's tough for them to bring up the subject and it can be tough for you to drop everything at a second's notice for a quick chat. But that's exactly what you need to do. This is no time to be prudish – if you want your kids to have accurate information and not to worry about sexual issues, you need to try and brush your own awkwardness aside and talk to them candidly.

Talking techniques

Your teen might have been building up to a chat for weeks. Alternatively, you might have been putting off talking to them about sex – there's always something more important to do, or it's never the right time. Well, life means it probably never will be the right time so you just have to take your chances when you can. Sometimes, a quick chat while you're making dinner or doing the school run can be far more natural and far less embarrassing for both parties than setting aside an hour for a more formal sit-down chat.

'Everyone gets embarrassed when talking about sex. And, if you happen to be talking to your own kids, the embarrassment on both sides is likely to be even more acute.'

Other options

If neither of you are comfortable sitting across a table chatting about sex then you need to come up with other ways to have the conversation. Perhaps you find eye contact difficult – if that's the case, why not have a chat in the car? Your teen can't escape if the topic gets tricky but you might find it easier to talk about certain subjects if you're not looking at each other. Or, you might prefer to go out somewhere public. That's not to say you have to share your conversation with diners in a crowded restaurant: you can pick a cosy table out of earshot but the hustle and bustle of a busy café can help to break up the tension and make it easier to open up.

Talking techniques checklist:

- Gen up on anything you're unsure of in advance.

- A lot of parents and kids find talking in the car helps when dealing with embarrassing topics – no need for eye contact.

- Don't shy away from tricky subjects.

- Go out for a walk or out for a coffee – sometimes it helps to be out of the house on neutral territory.

- Use TV characters or friends as examples, if you don't want to talk specifically about your child.

- If you both find it very difficult to talk, use other options – phone calls, texts, emails – whatever works to get the message across!

Body image problems

Most teens go through some kind of body image issues at some point – it's only natural. Your son might think he's too skinny and wants to bulk out more, or your daughter might be conscious of her curves and want to go back to her slimline, prepubescent shape. With so many changes occurring in such a short space of time, it's no surprise that these issues come up.

You might not be able to convince your kids that they're perfect just the way they are; that their spots will eventually disappear and they'll develop into their bodies, until they feel totally at ease. But regular reassurance and the benefit of your own teenage traumas and experience will help them to appreciate that they're not the only one going through it.

Keep your issues to yourself

If you have body image issues, try to keep these hidden from your teen. If you constantly talk about diets, your weight and your body, you're inevitably going to inflict a certain amount of your own image phobias onto your teen. They will have enough on their plate dealing with media bombardment, peer preconceptions about perfection and their own insecurities, without adding yours to the list.

Try to encourage healthy attitudes to food and weight from an early age and avoid talk of dieting to lose weight, or telling your child they're overweight. A good balance of healthy diet and exercise should be encouraged – any anxieties about food that children pick up on when they're young will be more likely to manifest themselves as they hit puberty.

Where to go for help and advice

If you're worried about your teen, you might be hesitant to ask other people for help. But there are plenty of charities and helplines dedicated to teen-specific issues. You'll find a list of useful names and contacts at the back of the book. Just remember, everyone is on your side and sometimes it's just reassuring to talk things through with an independent listener – someone outside of the situation who can offer impartial advice and perhaps get you to look at things in a different light.

Partner

Your partner should be your first port of call. Never keep a problem or a worry to yourself. Obviously, if your teen has spoken to you in complete confidence, you should respect their request, but you also need to weigh up the

'If you have body image issues, try to keep these hidden from your teen.'

importance of involving your partner in any big or difficult decisions. If you're a single parent but you still have close contact with your teen's other parent then you might want to consult them about certain issues.

School

If your teen is having problems at school, make an appointment to see the head teacher. You don't have to let your teen know you're doing this – unless they have asked you to. This is particularly important for bullying or sexual harassment, as things might need to be taken further. If the problem isn't addressed quickly and firmly, it can soon escalate.

Friends

Sometimes friends can offer another way of looking at situations. They may well know your teen, have kids themselves, or have experience of similar problems. As long as you're not divulging confidential information (and therefore jeopardising the trust of your teen), you can call on friends to give you advice.

'If your teen comes to you with a problem – anything from pregnancy to STIs – the most important thing you can do is not to judge them.'

What to do when your kids are in trouble

If your teen comes to you with a problem – anything from pregnancy to STIs – the most important thing you can do is not to judge them. The event (whatever it is) has happened now and, whilst you might be angry or hurt, this isn't the time for recriminations; it's the time to work through the problem and find a solution. Everyone makes mistakes and you have to hope that your teen learns from theirs and moves on. Take their opinions on board, give your own advice and come up with a plan of action.

What if your teen is pregnant?

If your daughter is pregnant, she'll need to think carefully about all the options open to her. If she decides to have a termination, this should be done as soon as possible, in order to minimise the discomfort of the procedure. Depending on the nature of the relationship with the father of the unborn child, you might want to involve him. However, the father doesn't have a right to say whether your daughter should keep or terminate the baby – that is solely her decision.

If your son's girlfriend is pregnant, you will probably want to consult with her and her family. At the end of the day, the final decision will be hers but you should offer support if possible, and encourage your son to face up to his responsibility and deal with the consequences. If he knows he has your support, he will be better able to deal with the situation. To help you deal with either situation, take a look at *Teenage Pregnancy – The Essential Guide*, Need2Know.

What if your child has an STI?

Once again, you need to put away your judgemental hat – the one with 'I told you so' written across the front – and try to provide independent help and advice. As soon as you suspect something is wrong, or your teen confides in you, you need to get them tested. It's quick and easy to diagnose most STIs and you can go to any sexual health clinic, or visit your family doctor if your teen is comfortable doing this.

You can pick up extra information on STIs while you're there – as the message might not have got through the first time around, and you'll be able to ask questions and get any extra sexual health advice that your teen needs. You could also take a look at another Need2Know book – *Sexually Transmitted Infections – The Essential Guide*.

Summing Up

- You need to overcome your embarrassment if you want to talk to your teen openly.

- Don't let your own body issues affect your teen. Promote a healthy lifestyle – not one based on binge diets.

- If you need advice, use all avenues open to you. Being a parent is a tough job – so don't be afraid to ask for help.

- Try and deal with problems in a rational way. Once a situation arises, it's too late for lecturing – now's the time for action and this is when your teen really needs your help.

Chapter Nine

Troubleshooting Guide for Parents

My teen won't talk to me

It can be difficult to get a teenager to talk about what they have done at school, let alone discuss intimate details about fragile first sexual encounters. You shouldn't be surprised if your teen refuses to talk about anything to do with sex the first time you raise the subject. But don't be despondent. By mentioning sex, you've shown that you're happy to talk about it and you're aware of the fact that they're maturing and reaching an age when sex might become a part of their life.

As mentioned in chapter 3, research has shown that 75% of British 11 to 14-year-olds do want to talk to their parents about sex; they just find it difficult (*Everyday Conversations, Every day*). So, you are thinking along the same lines as your kids, it's just a case of finding the right time and the place to have the conversations where you both feel relaxed enough to be open.

Give them time and space

Never try to push the issue: by all means gently enquire, drop hints and try to start conversations about sex, but whatever you do, don't pressurise your teen into talking. If they feel cajoled, they're more likely to clam up and distance themselves from you. The idea is to create a home environment that puts them at ease and allows them to open up and have frank discussions with you. Teenagers like to do things in their own good time and on their own terms.

'It can be difficult to get a teenager to talk about what they have done at school, let alone discuss intimate details about fragile first sexual encounters.'

Take time out

If you find it difficult to have tricky conversations, then why not set aside some time with your teen away from the house? The hustle and bustle of daily family life often leaves little time for one-to-ones. Whilst you might enjoy meals or television time together as a family, Sunday lunch is hardly the time or place to ask your teen if they're using contraception! Set aside some quality time and take them out on their own – shopping, lunch, cinema – whatever the setting, it will give you both a chance to open up and talk frankly to each other.

How do I bring sex up at home?

'If you find it difficult to have tricky conversations, then why not set aside some time with your teen away from the house?'

As we've already briefly discussed, there are certain times when it's a definite no-no to raise sex and relationship questions. You know when your kids are at their most receptive, and it really comes down to gut feeling and common sense as to when and where is the right time to talk. For example, you wouldn't stride into the living room, switch off the telly and begin a monologue about STIs.

Often, the topic will crop up naturally. You might be chatting to your teen about one of their friends having a new partner, or something that was mentioned at school, and this could provide the ideal opportunity to take the conversation further and find out if they have any questions or worries themselves. If you remind yourself that teens do want to talk, all you have to do is to make it easy for them to ask the questions.

Take your cue

Whilst friends and acquaintances can provide the impetus for discussions about sex and relationships, there are other ways to bring up the issues that you feel your teen should be made aware of. Television programmes often start discussions and a sensitive storyline can be a good way to raise the issue of sex at home. Likewise, the Internet, newspaper articles and radio phone-ins can provoke strong views and get you talking to your teen about sex.

Don't assume you have to build up to the big, 'let's sit down and talk about sex' scenario. Bite-sized chunks of information, informal chats and quick question times can be an equally good way to bring up sex at home. This will also make sure the conversations are ongoing and natural, and not just a dreaded one-off event.

I don't agree with sex before marriage or homosexuality

Everyone has – and is entitled to have – their own views about sex before marriage but, as a parent, you have the difficult job of trying to tone down your views to a certain extent. Whilst it's highly unlikely that you and your teen will see eye to eye on every issue, you'll get more out of them and will encourage a greater degree of mutual understanding and openness, if you accept their views rather than denouncing them and pressing home your own opinions about sex before marriage and sexuality.

Agree to disagree

This doesn't mean you have to go against your beliefs – in fact, good discussions can result from differing opinions – but being too steadfast and fixed in your views could alienate your teen and make them shy away from telling you anything they think you might disapprove of. Whether or not you approve of sex before marriage, the reality is that most young people are ambiguous at best about saving their virginity until they get married.

Gay relationships

As with sex before marriage, if you personally disapprove of homosexuality, you have to accept that your views are in the minority. Today, gay sex and relationships form an important part of sex education and no parent can make the assumption that their child is heterosexual. If your teen has grown up aware of your negative views on homosexuality, any experiences they have of same-sex relationships, experimentation or coming out as gay, will be far more difficult to discuss.

Listen without judgement

It can take a lot of courage for a teen to 'come out', and it will be an even braver move if your child is aware of your negative views about homosexuality. Most parents who have no idea about their child's sexuality will be shocked, to a certain extent, to learn that their son or daughter is gay. However, it's important to remember that they're still your child – they haven't changed, this has always been part of them, it has just taken them a while to be comfortable and confident enough with their sexuality to tell you.

Of course, you should talk to your child about your own concerns – be honest with them. Parents generally want the best for their kids and it might take you a while to adjust to the fact that your child is gay. You might have well-founded concerns about bullying or prejudice; you might have health concerns; or you might be naïve about aspects of homosexuality and just need some reassurance from your child – or an independent group – to find out about how you can support your child.

I found a condom in their room

Most parents would be upset to discover evidence of their kid's sexual activity. Whether or not you're aware that your teen is having sex with a partner, it might still come as a shock to find out that it's going on under your own roof. But, however angry or upset you might be, never confront them immediately. Wait until you have calmed down and thought about the situation rationally. If you tackle them about it straight away, you won't have a chance to think through your own views on the subject. You are more likely to create a confrontational situation, which is of no benefit to either you or your teen. What could be a sensible discussion is more likely to be a heated argument.

Talk it through

If there's another parent in the household, talk to them about it first and work out an agreed approach on how you're going to deal with the discovery. It's always best to get another viewpoint but you should always try to come across as a united front when you actually come to talk to your teen about it. They need to know that both parents feel the same and they aren't getting mixed messages.

Crossing the boundaries

It's likely that you'll feel let down by the discovery, but teenage impulses don't always allow for the feelings of their parents, so try not to let this cloud your judgement of the bigger issue, which is your teen having sex in your house.

The proof is also proof of contraception

Whatever your views on your teen having sex in your home, the fact that you have discovered a condom means they're not having unprotected sex. This is such an important issue for youngsters to understand and to actually implement that any discussion on the subject should acknowledge that, although you find their behaviour disrespectful or upsetting, you appreciate that they are taking precautions against pregnancy and STIs.

Maybe they wanted you to find it

If the discovery of a condom has really upset and shaken you, remember it's a natural reaction, especially for parents who had no idea that their teen was engaging in sexual activity. But, also stop and think whether your teen might have wanted you to find it. It could be that it's a sign of provocation but, on the other hand, it could be a message that highlights the lack of parental involvement in their sex education. If you've been burying your head in the sand and avoiding any conversations about sex with your kids, then this will be a rude awakening. Whilst it's not the best way to drop a hint that you need to talk to your teen, take it as a message that it's time for a chat.

I worry my teen has an STI

It can be extremely difficult to tell if your teen has an STI. Some STIs, such as chlamydia and – to a certain extent – gonorrhoea, have no outward symptoms, or very subtle signs, but they can have serious long-term health repercussions. The good news is that most STIs are curable with a simple course of antibiotics.

'Teenage impulses don't always allow for the feelings of their parents.'

Broaching the subject

If you're worried that your teen has an STI, that means you're pretty sure they've had unprotected sex. This also means that the contraception message hasn't got through and, whether or not they have an STI, you need to sit them down for some serious sex advice. Instead of confronting them directly with your fears, why not suggest a routine check-up at the sexual health clinic? They can get tested but they will also be able to get detailed information about STIs. It might well be a bit more of a wake-up call than a cosy chat with Mum or Dad.

My child is watching porn

'Whether or not you've discussed sex and relationships openly with them, peer pressure and a natural curiosity means that they're likely to seek out pornography at some stage.'

It's a scenario that many parents will be familiar with: you're tidying up your teen's room, you glance at the computer and see that they've been looking at pornography. Or, you walk in and find them watching a pornographic film on television. Unfortunately, however much you disapprove of, or disagree with it, there's little you can do to erase pornography completely from their life, if they're determined to watch it.

It's perfectly normal

First of all, ask yourself why your teen is watching porn. Puberty, hormones, sexual awakening and a changing physical and emotional state are fairly justifiable reasons for a teenager to become increasingly curious about sex. So it follows that they will look to a number of different sources to answer their questions. Whether or not you've discussed sex and relationships openly with them, peer pressure and a natural curiosity means that they're likely to seek out pornography at some stage.

The age of technology

A generation ago, you could have confiscated their stash of top-shelf magazines, or moved the television out of their room. But these days, it's virtually impossible to protect your child from pornographic imagery. With computers, smart phones, tablets and other devices that link quickly and easily to the Internet, there is ample opportunity for teens to gain access to as much pornography as they want.

Dealing with the situation

As with all matters relating to your teen's sexual awakening, you should try and tread carefully and view the situation from their inexperienced perspective.

How to deal with it checklist:

- Don't invite conflict by allowing personal feelings about pornography to cloud your judgement.

- Explain your position – you might find it offensive or degrading, or you simply don't want them to be exposed to hardcore pornography.

- Explain how excessive exposure to pornography might give them a distorted view of gender roles in sexual relationships.

- Put parental locks on the Internet.

- Move computers to communal family areas to discourage the viewing of pornography at home.

Should I let their partner stay overnight?

This is a tricky issue and one that can create disharmony between parents and teens. Every parent knows that teenagers can and will have sex if they want to, but somehow the idea of them having sex in your own house makes the whole situation more difficult to accept.

Strong views

People often have one of two very distinct views on girlfriends or boyfriends staying in the family home:

- I don't want it going on in my house.

- If they're going to have sex anyway, I'd rather they did it somewhere safe and secure.

The argument against

The first view is generally based on strong moral or religious views and it can be difficult to convey your own beliefs to your children. Without generalising, each generation usually becomes more liberal in their views and your kids might think nothing of sleeping with their partner at home, whilst the thought of it makes you extremely uncomfortable. Aside from your own personal or moral viewpoint, there are many other reasons that you might say no:

- You might be embarrassed about what friends or family would think.

- You assume that this won't be their only relationship and you don't want to set a precedent for every time they meet a new partner.

- You might have concerns about setting the wrong example for younger siblings or the questions it might raise for young children.

At the end of the day, you have the final say about who stays in your house and what goes on there. If you feel strongly against boyfriends or girlfriends staying over, then you need to talk to your teen about this. It's a good idea to try and raise the issue well in advance of the question actually being asked, so everyone knows where they stand. Once you can see that a relationship is getting serious, you can let them know that you wouldn't be happy with their partner staying the night. Chances are, however, they will already know your views on the subject, as it may well have cropped up in conversation in relation to their friends or other people you know.

'It's extremely unlikely that the first person your teen dates is going to be the person they settle down with, so think of the early dating years as an experiment.'

I worry that their partner is a bad influence

Parents rarely think partners are worthy of their kids; it's just a fact of life. But there comes a point when you need to accept that teens will make their own mistakes – as you did – and each experience as they grow up will shape their personality and make them stronger.

It's extremely unlikely that the first person your teen dates is going to be the person they settle down with, so think of the early dating years as an experiment. They might go for people you view as the 'wrong type' to get attention, to annoy you, to impress their friends, or just to rebel. Most teens quickly realise that it's no fun dating someone who is unreliable, sleeps around or disrespects them and, chances are, your teen will find their dating feet and become pickier about partners as they get older.

Be supportive

If you take an immediate dislike to your teen's new partner, the last thing you should do is to list their faults and tell your teen they're not good enough or they're a bad influence. The teenage years are the rebellion period, and provocation will be like fanning a fire. Your teen will soon pick up on your ambivalence towards their partner; they'll get the hint without you having to spell it out. Just play the waiting game and, in most instances, they will work out for themselves that their partner isn't worth hanging on to. In which case, be ready and waiting with a box of tissues and open arms when the relationship ends.

If all else fails

If your concerns are based on fact and you know that their new partner has been in trouble with the police, has numerous other partners, has unprotected sex or is seriously influencing your son or daughter in a negative way, then you might need to intervene.

- Try talking to your teen about their partner – ask how much they really know about them.

- Tell your teen that you don't like the way their partner speaks to them/treats them: they deserve to be treated with more respect.

- Present them with facts if you have them.

- If your teen and their partner are at school or college, talk to the head teacher about your concerns.

- Reiterate rules about behaviour and the consequences for breaking the rules: always keep them focused on the limits you have set.

My daughter wants a baby

If you've hammered home the importance of contraception, the dangers of catching STIs and the choices your teen needs to make about when they choose to have sex and who with, you probably think that you have done as much as you can to prepare your teen for sex and relationships. But, what do you do if your daughter actually wants a baby and is actively trying to get pregnant?

Make sure she's prepared

It might well be a phase, so don't panic just yet. It could be that she's fallen head over heels in love with a new boyfriend and thinks the next natural stage is to have a baby. Or maybe she has a maternal urge that she feels will only be fulfilled by having her own child. Whatever the reason, the first thing you need to do is to give her all the facts. If you have friends or relatives with babies, take her to visit and get a sense of the realities of caring for a newborn. It's not all nursery rhymes and tiny babygros: you need to make sure that she's aware of all the things she'll be giving up if she decides to have a baby at this stage in her life:

- Further education.
- Socialising.
- Career plans for the immediate future.
- Financial independence.

The pressures of parenthood

Very young parents are often put under greater strains than those who have children later on. This doesn't mean that their parenting skills are lacking; but it can be more difficult to maintain a relationship if both parties are young and inexperienced. The sudden transition from carefree teen to responsible parent can put immense pressure on the new parents and this, combined with financial worries and being cut off from the lifestyles of their peers, means teen parents need solid family support.

Could your son or daughter cope if you didn't help out with childcare, housing or money? It might just be a hypothetical question but ask them and see if they still think it's a good idea to become a parent at such a young age.

Summing Up

▨ Let your teen come to you: don't pressure them into talking about sex.

▨ Give it time – don't bring up the subject on a daily basis.

▨ Use television programmes and newspaper stories to start discussions about sex in a natural and familiar environment.

▨ If home life is hectic, take your teen out for some quality time and a heart to heart.

▨ Deal with pornography sensitively and explain your views in a rational way.

▨ Discuss your views on overnight stays in advance of the question arising.

▨ If you're worried about STIs, get your teen tested.

▨ If your daughter wants a baby, present her with the realities of bringing up a child.

Chapter Ten

Bigger Problems

Coping with pregnancy

The discovery that your daughter is pregnant (or that your son is going to be a father) will be an emotional time for all involved. If the pregnancy was unplanned you may well feel anger or disappointment with your teen for taking such a miscalculated risk.

Deciding what to do

Pregnancy doesn't have to make you or your teen powerless. You do have options and it's important to discuss them all in detail before your teen makes a final decision about what to do. As a parent, this is the time to offer support: it's too late for reprimands.

Termination

By law, in the United Kingdom a woman can terminate an unwanted pregnancy up to 24 weeks. Whilst some people know immediately that they want to terminate their pregnancy, for others it's a difficult decision to make but the option that they ultimately choose, rather than going ahead with an unplanned pregnancy. There are many things to consider when you talk to your teen about their options: is the father of the baby on the scene, or is the relationship over? Has she told the father, or is she intending to? If so, what are his views on the pregnancy? You might also consider the age of your teen, and her personal circumstances.

'Pregnancy doesn't have to make you or your teen powerless.'

It is worth taking into account the different methods of termination which are used at different stages of the pregnancy. If your teen does decide to go ahead with a termination then it is best to arrange the procedure as soon as possible. As the pregnancy continues, the termination is more intrusive, and it will also become more difficult to conceal the pregnancy. A good source of information is *Abortion – The Essential Guide*, Need2Know.

What happens next

If you are planning to have an abortion through the NHS, you must be referred by two doctors, who agree that an abortion is the right course of action for the woman's physical or mental health. If you choose to go to a private clinic, you don't need the doctors' referrals but you will have to pay for the procedure. If the pregnancy is less than nine weeks the procedure is quick and involves a pill rather than surgery. After nine weeks, the suction method is necessary but again, it is a very quick procedure. After 15 weeks, a surgical abortion will be required, and this involves staying in hospital overnight.

Keeping the baby

Termination isn't an option for everyone. Many people dismiss it outright, due to religious or moral reasons. If your teen has decided to keep her baby, then there is plenty of support for teenage mums. In fact, it makes sense for both you and your teen to get some independent and impartial advice at this stage. Brook Advisory Service offers confidential advice to under 25s on everything to do with sex and relationships, so this would be good place to start. See the help list.

Planning ahead

If there's going to be a new addition to the family, you'll need to discuss living arrangements, childcare and education well in advance. If your daughter is still in school or college then talk to the school about her options and whether it's possible to take some time out and return at a later date to continue studying.

With regards to living arrangements, you'll need to think about where your daughter and her new baby are going to live. If she is in a relationship with the father, involve him and his parents too at this stage. Here's some questions for everyone to consider:

- Are the couple going to live together, or does it make more sense for your daughter and the baby to live with you initially?

- Do you have the space and are there other children in the household? Their needs should also be taken into consideration.

- How is she going to manage financially? Will you support her or do you feel she should be financially independent?

- How much support will you give her? For example, will you offer childcare so she can continue studying? If you have work or other commitments, you need to make it clear that you won't be available for ad hoc babysitting.

Cyberbullying

Every generation has a new set of technologies to deal with, but teens today have perhaps taken the greatest technological leap in decades. As parents, you were probably thrilled to have a television with a few channels to choose from and maybe a very basic computer. Nowadays however, children are bombarded with information from numerous sources on a daily basis. It is much more difficult to keep track of what your kids are up to and who they're mixing with, when they have their own mobile phones, laptops, and social networking accounts.

The secret life of teens

Gone are the days when teens had to whisper into the landline phone when they wanted to have a private conversation with their friends. They can now text, picture message and chat online while they're sitting in the same room as you watching television, and you won't necessarily have a clue who they're talking to, or what they're talking about, looking at or listening to. This can cause huge problems when it comes to bullying and intimidation. Where once

'Every generation has a new set of technologies to deal with, but teens today have perhaps taken the greatest technological leap in decades.'

altercations took place in public, in the school playground or the local park, bullying has moved on with technology and there are now countless new ways for bullies to create an environment of fear and intimidation.

Online slander

Rumours spread far more quickly in cyberspace than they do in the physical world and a reputation can be tarnished in the click of a button. Bullies have been quick on the uptake when it comes to using chat rooms and social networking sites to humiliate their victims. The truth of rumours is secondary to the distress that they cause, and scores are often settled in chat rooms these days, with bitchy comments, sexual slander and retaliations taking place online, in front of schoolmates, friends and casual observers. Whilst a caustic remark in the playground will only be heard by a handful of people, a comment in a chat room can be read by thousands.

'Sexting is when people send and receive explicit images on their mobile phones.'

Sexting

Some parents might not even be aware of the term 'sexting', let alone realise that their kids are involved in it. Sexting is when people send and receive explicit images on their mobile phones. Most mobiles have cameras and picture messaging functions so in theory, any teen can produce or receive these images. This technology on tap obviously makes sharing pornography extremely easy but, more worryingly, it makes it easy for teens to share pornographic images of themselves. Teens will often send images to their partners, or to impress each other and make themselves more attractive to prospective partners.

As with cyberbullying, sexual images can very quickly be distributed to a large number of people, and the sender has no control over where the image will eventually end up. Whilst many teens regard this practice of texting sexual images as harmless fun between friends, it can have long-term repercussions. These images could turn up online, on social networking sites, or passed around the entire school. What began as a prank could quickly become a humiliation. The trouble is that teenagers often live for the present and any advice you offer needs to take this into account: you need to try to make them understand that these images will be around forever.

98

It's very difficult to offer impartial advice on something that seems so blindingly obvious to an adult but, if you want your teen to take your advice on board, it's vital that you don't come across as being judgemental. You could try asking rhetorical questions: this will encourage them to regard the scenario from an objective perspective.

- Are you confident your boyfriend/girlfriend won't send these images to their friends?
- Do you want strangers to see sexually provocative images of you?
- What if your friends' parents saw them? How would you feel?
- Would you like a future boyfriend/girlfriend to know about this?
- What impression do you think these images give to other people?

The pressure to have sex

This pressure can come from partners or peers, but also from more unlikely sources like films and television programmes, or celebrity role models. Teens like to fit in, so those who have already lost their virginity will be busy trying to encourage everyone else to do likewise, whilst those who haven't had sex yet feel like they're missing out. Boys and girls naturally have different views about sex but they can all be too eager to embark on sexual relationships, so the addition of peer pressure can make it very difficult to resist. It takes strength of character, confidence and maturity to resist the constant pressure, and many teens find this part of growing up particularly challenging.

Reassure your teen

If you think your teen is being pressurised into having sex, either by their partner or their peers, you should broach the subject with them. All sexual activity should be undertaken through choice. If your teen feels the momentous decision to lose their virginity is not entirely of their own making, this could have repercussions for future relationships and certainly for their feelings of self-worth and confidence. It's important to emphasise that they have to reach the decision of their own accord and, armed with all their knowledge and personal experience, this is a decision that only they can make.

The pressure to sleep around

In the same way that teens put pressure on each other to have sex, they also goad each other about their number of sexual partners. Whilst a lot of this is exaggerated, it can make persuasive listening for the sexually inexperienced. If your son or daughter has a girlfriend or boyfriend then they will probably be 'let off the hook' by their friends as cheating on a partner doesn't have quite the bravado factor as sleeping around. However, teen relationships – especially early on – can be short-lived and fickle and there is a constant pressure to meet someone new, or sleep with the next person on the list.

Of course, there are meaningful teenage relationships and it's not unheard of for a relationship that is formed during teenage years to lead to a long-term or life partnership. But, in most cases, those first relationships form the stumbling ground and building blocks of sexual and emotional relationship experience. With hormones raging and emotions scattered all over the place, the odds are stacked against long-term relationships at this age, and the emphasis is often placed on the number of sexual partners, rather than looking for long-term love.

Teenagers use these experiences to learn about intimacy, trust and sexual behaviour, as well as developing their own character and personality and discovering more about themselves and what they want from a relationship. Mistakes are made, hearts are broken and feelings are explored – as a parent you need to be there to offer unconditional love and support, as well an empathetic shoulder to cry on.

Harassment and sexual abuse

Whatever choices your teen makes with regards to sexual relationships, there is always the possibility of their being harassed or, worse, sexually abused. If you notice any sudden changes in your child's behaviour – they may become withdrawn, sullen, quiet or unexpectedly emotional – you must address the issue straight away. Perhaps you already have concerns about a new boyfriend or girlfriend, or maybe your teen has got in with the wrong crowd. Although unpleasant, peer pressure to have sex is a very different situation to sexual harassment. If your teen is getting unwanted sexual attention, is being plagued with sexually explicit text messages or images, or is being taunted in a sexual way at school, the situation is going to require more than a shoulder to cry on.

Sexual harassment can be an incredibly frightening experience and it's likely that your teen will need professional counselling to deal with the trauma. There are a number of helplines and organisations that deal specifically with sexual harassment and abuse, including Rape & Sexual Abuse Support Centre, and Parents Protect. See the help list. These could be good starting points for your teen to get independent support, and for you, as their parent, to get advice about how to deal with their experiences.

There are specific laws in the UK relating to harassment, such as the Protection from Harassment Act 1997, so don't be afraid to discuss the matter with the police. Minor instances of harassment can soon escalate if they are not dealt with, and the perpetrators thrive on their victim's fear and the belief that they won't report the incident. Don't let your teen become a victim: sexual harassment is a crime.

- Talk to your teen and find out exactly what's going on.

- Make an appointment with the appropriate person at their school to discuss the situation.

- If the harassment is outside of school, it might be a matter for the police.

- Change their phone number and email addresses and encourage them to remove their profile from social networking sites.

'Sexual harassment can be an incredibly frightening experience and it's likely that your teen will need professional counselling to deal with the trauma.'

Summing Up

- If your teen is pregnant, discuss all her options with her.

- Get some independent advice about pregnancy before you come to any decisions about what to do.

- If your daughter chooses to have a termination, book an appointment as soon as you can.

- If she chooses to keep the baby, discuss living arrangements, parental responsibilities and the amount of help you are willing and able to offer.

- Keep up to date with technology and take an active interest in what your teen is watching online.

- Talk to them candidly about cyberbullying and the implications of passing round provocative images of themselves.

- Encourage your teen to think independently about their sexual choices and not to be swayed by peer pressure.

Help List

Barnardo's

www.barnardos.org.uk

A great reference for parents, covering all elements of raising kids.

Brook Advisory Service

Tel: 0808 802 1234

www.brook.org.uk

Confidential help and advice for young people on all aspects of sexual health and relationship issues.

Divorce Aid

www.divorceaid.co.uk

This online resource has plenty of specific help pages for kids whose parents are going through divorce.

Family Lives

Tel: 0808 800 2222

www.familylives.org.uk

The place for parents to get advice on all aspects of family life. Call the helpline any time – open seven days a week.

FFLAG (Families and Friends of Lesbians and Gays)

PO Box 495, Little Stoke, Bristol, BS34 9AP

Tel: 0845 652 0311

www.fflag.org.uk

Young gay and lesbian people and their friends and family can get support here.

FPA (Family Planning Association)

Tel: 0845 122 8690 (England)
Tel: 0845 122 8687 (Northern Ireland)
www.fpa.org.uk
A great resource for all issues relating to sexual health, from contraception to teenage pregnancy.

Gingerbread

Tel: 0808 802 0925
www.gingerbread.org.uk
Advice for single parents – you'll find help on everything from money issues to raising teens.

Kidscape

020 7730 3300
www.kidscape.org.uk
If your child is being bullied and they need independent support, or you feel unable to cope as a parent, Kidscape can help.

Marie Stopes Clinics

Tel: 0845 300 8090 (24 hours)
www.mariestopes.org.uk
Supportive advice on abortion and sexual health issues.

Parents Protect

Tel: 0808 1000 900
www.parentsprotect.co.uk
Information and advice on how to keep children safe from sexual abuse, as well as help for those who have suffered sexual abuse.

Rape Crisis

Tel: 0808 802 9999
www.rapecrisis.org.uk
If your teen has been raped or sexually abused, Rape Crisis can offer support and advice.

Rape & Sexual Abuse Support Centre

Tel: 0808 802 9999
www.rasasc.org.uk
Independent help and advice for anyone who has been the victim of rape or sexual abuse.

Relate for Parents

www.relateforparents.org.uk
Online relationship advice for families, offering support to all members of the family unit.

UK Parent Coaching

www.ukparentcoaching.co.uk
An online resource for parents looking for help with improving their relationship with their kids.

Bibliography

Everyday Conversations, Every Day, Teenage Pregnancy Independent Advisory Service (TPIAG), June 2008

Sex and Relationship Education Guidance, published by DfES, July 2000

Populus, June 2008

United Nations Statistics (Indicators on Childbearing, 2009)

ONS (Office for National Statistics), 2011

  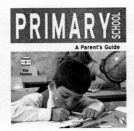  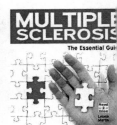